Pro-Style Bodybuilding

Pro-Style Bodybuilding

By Tom Platz with Bill Reynolds

Foreword by Arnold Schwarzenegger

 Sterling Publishing Co., Inc.   New York

Edited by Robert Hernandez

Designed by Jim Anderson

Photo Credits:
All photos by John Balik unless otherwise credited.

Library of Congress Cataloging in Publication Data

Platz, Tom.
   Pro-style bodybuilding.

   Includes index.
   1. Bodybuilding. I. Reynolds, Bill II. Title.
GV546.5.P57 1985   646.7′5   84-23950
ISBN 0-8069-4188-X
ISBN 0-8069-7910-0 (pbk.)

Contents

Foreword 6
by Arnold Schwarzenegger

Introduction 8

Chapter 1 Basic Training 10
Strategies

Chapter 2 Off-Season 28
Diet

Chapter 3 Training Factors 34
for the Off-Season

Chapter 4 Off-Season Exercises 42
& Routines

Chapter 5 Precontest 92
Training Tips

Chapter 6 Diet for the 104
Competitive Edge

Chapter 7 Precontest Exercises 110
& Routines

Chapter 8 Winning Mental 156
Approach

Chapter 9 Bodybuilding 164
Competition

Chapter 10 The Learning 184
Process

Index 190

Foreword

I am pleased to write this foreword to Tom Platz's new book, *Pro-Style Bodybuilding*, because Tom's physique is what bodybuilding is all about in the 1980s. So far, he is the only athlete who has distinguished himself from bodybuilding as it was in my own era during the 1970s.

Bodybuilding has constantly progressed since its true competitive beginnings in the early 1940s. Then they had herculean bodybuilders who were not very muscular and didn't have balanced proportions. In the 1950s and 1960s, bodybuilders like Reg Park and Bill Pearl added great proportions to this type of physique. In the 1970s, bodybuilders became muscularly dense. Not only were they perfectly developed overall, they were also perfect within each body part. A tall guy with a big chest and massive arms couldn't just walk in and win a show any longer.

Tom has added an extra dimension to his physique. He has developed the ultimate degree of thickness and muscular definition. The bodybuilders of my era never had Tom's size and hardness because we didn't have the sophisticated training methods that he has developed. Tom's not finished with a set until he knows he simply can't move the weight another inch. With this principle and his dietary expertise, he's taken physical development to the logical limit.

Tom is extremely inspirational to hundreds of thousands of young bodybuilders who weren't born tall and weren't blessed with the most perfect proportions. Tom didn't initially have them, but through intelligent training he was able to create perfect proportions. He is the ultimate inspiration to young guys out there who are not six feet two inches tall with wide shoulders and a narrow waist, but who can perfect their bodies through hard work.

I am impressed with how much time Tom puts back into the sport, acting as one of bodybuilding's best ambassadors. He does scores of training seminars to help promote bodybuilding. High-level bodybuilding always indicates a certain degree of selfishness—as does every sport—because you have to say no to people to gain time for your training and other preparations. But unlike other bodybuilders who spend all of their time in the gym, Tom Platz has been able to devote time to others. He is *always* willing to support bodybuilding.

Tom is one of the most sensitive and intelligent bodybuilders around today because he knows both his weak and strong points and trains accordingly. By ignoring his strong points and concentrating all of his energies on his weak points, Tom balanced his physique faster than anyone I've ever seen.

I feel that Tom has the potential to be as dominant competitively in the 1980s as I was in the 1970s. When you have substance, you will eventually end up on top. It will take many years for someone to reach Tom's level of development.

Training and nutritional expertise aside, I feel that it's Tom's mental intensity that most separates him from the masses of other bodybuilders fighting towards the top. I was noted for my own mental intensity, but Tom has taken his level of intensity miles down the road. He knows that it's more necessary for him to be intense because he wasn't born with my genetic structure.

Tom Platz has taken up where I left off and has become my successor in competitive bodybuilding. More power to him!

ARNOLD SCHWARZENEGGER
Mr. Universe (five times), Mr. World, Mr. Olympia (seven times), award-winning actor, best-selling author.

Introduction

I am a professional bodybuilder, and I couldn't be happier with my life. In this book, I hope to share with you some of the excitement of bodybuilding and give you an inside glimpse of how the champions of the sport have developed their outstanding bodies. More particularly, I will tell you exactly how I train, diet, and prepare myself mentally for major professional bodybuilding competitions.

I have organized this book in three major areas. The first of these is concerned with the off-season cycle. In Chapter 1, I discuss basic training strategies; Chapter 2 covers the off-season diet; Chapter 3 focusses on important off-season training factors; and in Chapter 4, I give you more than 20 key exercises and several off-season training routines, including my own off-season program.

The second section of this book deals with precontest training strategies. In Chapter 5, I elaborate on precontest training strategies; Chapter 6 concentrates on the precontest diet; and in Chapter 7, I present more than 20 additional bodybuilding exercises and a great variety of precontest training programs.

The final section of this book is concerned with the overall aspects of bodybuilding. Chapter 8 covers one of my favorite topics, the winning mental approach; Chapter 9 is a look at the ins and outs of bodybuilding competitions; and in Chapter 10, I finish with the total learning process in bodybuilding.

This book is primarily intended for advanced bodybuilders who are preparing themselves for competitions. That's not to say that beginners and intermediates won't get a lot out of the book, but they will definitely need to read a beginning-level bodybuilding book before tackling this text. Without an introduction to the basics of the sport, it would be difficult to understand much of the material here.

I can make you one promise before you begin exploring my concepts of serious bodybuilding: If you follow my advice to the letter, you *will* improve. I can't promise that you'll win Mr. Olympia, because you may not have the potential to win such an exalted title. But you will improve. Let's go for it!

Tom Platz
Mr. Universe

1 Basic Training Strategies

Off-season training in competitive bodybuilding is the time when you build all of your muscle mass and increase your power in each exercise. Then, during a peaking cycle, you strip all of the fat from your body to reveal the well-defined muscles that you've built up in the off-season.

In terms of muscular development, you should actually have two objectives in the off-season: to generally increase muscle mass and to particularly develop any lagging body parts. When you are preparing for a major competition, you simply can't do anything to bring up a weak point because you aren't consuming enough calories to train any muscle group with sufficient intensity to increase its mass. Therefore, all champion bodybuilders—myself included—blast a weak muscle group to the limit during the off-season in order to bring it up to par with the rest of the physique.

Identifying Weak Points

After a major competition, such as the Mr. Olympia show, I will closely analyze my physique to identify strong and weak points. Since I have been a competitive bodybuilder for many years, I can do this quite objectively. If you are new to the sport, it might be best to seek out an unbiased expert to help you evaluate your physique. Probably the best person for this task is a judge who has already evaluated you in a competition. If you approach one politely and with a willingness to learn, he or she can give you valuable feedback.

Some gym owners and most champion bodybuilders can also provide good sources of feedback about your physique. However, I would avoid asking the opinion of your gym buddies, who for the most part will feel you can do nothing wrong in the sport. They are likely to be the people who will slap you on the back, even though you don't have a back muscle to your name, and tell you that you're good enough to beat Platz, Bannout, Haney, Schwarzenegger, and every other top bodybuilder in history.

When I evaluate myself after a major show, I don't use a mirror that often. Photographs, videotapes, and the criticism of individuals whose opinions I respect are invaluable to me. I find videotapes of particular interest because they reveal my physique in actual motion. Unfortunately, I've seldom had access to video feedback and must rely heavily on photographs.

Before, during, and after a major championship, I am photographed hundreds of times by the lensmen who work for *Muscle & Fitness* magazine, and I carefully analyze every photo. I also receive literally hundreds of photos in the mail from my fans, each of which is also put under close scrutiny. Often one of my fans will send me a photo that I simply hate to look at, but this type of photo is most valuable to me. It graphically reveals some weakness in either my physical development or my posing ability which becomes the first thing that I attack when I have completed my evaluation procedure.

Muscle-Priority Training

Once you have identified a weak muscle group that must be improved upon in the off-season, I firmly believe that you must attack the muscle both mentally and physically. I'll think hard about what I am lacking and which basic area I want to concentrate on most. And you must understand that you will have different weak points from year to year because various body parts improve more or less quickly than others.

In my own case, my biceps and triceps needed additional development one year, so I put priority on training my arms. Another year I was more concerned with improving my back development. This isn't to say that I slacked off on training other areas; it's just that I became more concerned with the weaker body part, particularly in regard to mental concentration. (I discuss my mental approach to bodybuilding in Chapter 8.)

If you have a weak muscle group, it's essential that you train it first in your workout when you have maximum mental and physical energy to devote to bombing it to the limit. And training a weak point to the max is where it's at in bodybuilding. I will never leave the gym until I have done everything I possibly can to stress a weak muscle group to the limit.

During an off-season cycle, I will arrange my workouts so I can attack my weak area first. It is also possible to plan your workouts so you train a weak group by itself and the remainder of your body on a separate day. I haven't personally used this plan, but I feel it would work particularly well for those bodybuilders who need leg development. With this version of muscle-priority training, you could do just thigh work one day, then follow it up with a workout for the remainder of your body the next day. This is precisely the training plan that the legendary Lou Ferrigno used during his late-teen years when his thighs were not balanced with his upper body.

I follow a five-day workout cycle in the off-season, training four straight

days, taking one day of rest, and then renewing the cycle. I've arranged my workouts so I essentially exercise one large muscle group and one small body part each training session. The first day I do chest and rear delts, back and side delts the second day, just arms the third day, and legs the fourth day. Because I tore a biceps tendon in a freak injury a year ago, my arms are currently my priority group, and training biceps and triceps by themselves allows me to work them with maximum intensity, which in turn forces them to grow in mass and strength very quickly.

I'll talk about how to physically increase the intensity of off-season workouts for lagging body parts in this chapter, but you *must* understand that my mental intensity in this case is the driving force behind my actual workouts. When I am specializing on a weak body part, I don't necessarily do more sets or use more weight—although to some extent this does naturally occur—but rather I consciously realize what I need to improve and focus all of my mental attention on it. This mental intensity is the true key to bringing up a lagging body part to the level of the rest of your physique.

Just to show you how powerful the mind is in the bodybuilding process, I'll tell you about two competitions I entered early in my career. For the first one, I dieted and trained perfectly and was mentally into the process, and I ended up looking both huge and ripped. Then the next time I competed, I dieted and trained precisely the same as the first time, but due to some unexpected pressures at school was unable to maintain a good mental focus on the upcoming show. And when I competed, my physique looked as though I hadn't even prepared for it. Even though I'd been eating only fish and chicken, my body looked

as though I'd been on a diet of jelly doughnuts! The human mind is that powerful, so you must always use it to your advantage in bodybuilding.

Off-Season Power Training

It is an incontrovertible fact that strong muscles are big muscles. To put it another way, the heavier the weights you lift for several reps in an exercise, the larger the muscles will be that contract to move the weight. Therefore, all champion bodybuilders train as heavily as they can in strict form, using basic exercises, during an off-season cycle.

Some champion bodybuilders actually compete at a high level in powerlifting during their off-season cycles. I was a powerlifter for a couple of years just before I began to make my mark at the national level in bodybuilding. Scott Wilson (Mr. International, Pro Mr. America, and a Pro Grand Prix Champion) holds a Master's rating in powerlifting, and Dr. Franco Columbu (twice Mr. Olympia) was a European champion who set several world records in powerlifting.

While a minority of superstar bodybuilders compete in powerlifting or weightlifting meets, all of the most massive champs are phenomenally strong. To give you a few examples, Arnold Schwarzenegger (seven-time Mr. Olympia) has performed a deadlift with 750 pounds; Lou Ferrigno (twice Mr. Universe) bench-presses with 550 pounds; Casey Viator (the youngest Mr. America) incline-presses with nearly 500 pounds; Lee Haney (Mr. America, Mr. Universe, and a leading pro bodybuilder) can do barbell bent rows with 400 pounds; Bertil Fox (three-time Mr. Universe) does eight reps in the seated-press-behind-neck movement with 335 pounds. I recently

Tom believes in heavy off-season power training on basic exercises to build massive muscles. Here he reps out with 500-pound deadlifts. (*Craig Dietz*)

had Gold's Gym purchase a pair of 180-pound dumbbells so I could toss around a little heavier iron in my incline dumbbell press.

I hope I've convinced you that you have to train for power in the off-season if you truly desire to build huge, ripped-to-shreds muscles. And the best way to train for strength without running the risk of injury is to pyramid your weights and reps on each basic exercise that you use in your power workouts. In a true pyramid, you should add weight to the bar and progressively reduce the number of reps you perform with each succeeding set of an exercise. Repeat the process in the opposite direction by removing weight and increasing your reps each set until you return to the starting point. However, I have always used and highly recommend a half pyramid in which you work up in weight and down in reps until you reach your peak poundage, then drop back for only one or two high-rep sets.

The following is an example of how you could pyramid your weights and reps in the bench press (the weights listed have been arbitrarily chosen only for the sake of illustration):

Set Number	Weight (lbs.)	Reps
1	135	12
2	165	10
3	195	8
4	215	6
5	235	4
6	250	2
7	185	maximum

If you are prone to injury, you should probably go no lower than three to five reps on each set, and you should definitely avoid doing single repetitions to show off your strength to your gym mates. Even if you have never had a problem with injuries, you should never attempt to lift an unusually heavy weight (a "limit single effort") more frequently than once every two or three weeks.

For bodybuilders, limit singles in any exercise are of very little value beyond a brief ego gratification. It has been determined that single reps build no muscle mass, just muscle contractile force and greater strength in ligaments, tendons, and other connective tissues. And the risk of injury when trying to hit a max single is greatly magnified. Even if you don't incur a traumatic injury that is immediately painful, very heavy single lifts can initiate a degenerative condition of the articulating surfaces of your body's major joints. However, moderately heavy weights lifted in perfect form for more than two or three reps following a good warm-up will not harm your joints, and they *will* build massive muscles.

This last fact hits at the core value of using a pyramid system in your off-season workouts. A good pyramid allows you to warm up thoroughly before you attack the heavy, musclebuilding sets of six, four, and two reps. Used with basic exercises, pyramid-power training to muscle failure (and often past the point of failure) and working out consistently (all of which are explained in greater detail later in this chapter) can give you an astounding physique.

Over the years, I've observed that bodybuilders can increase their training poundages beyond their wildest dreams. The first time I arranged my reps and poundages in a pyramid in my squat workouts, I added 10–15 pounds per week to each set for almost six months, which resulted in an unbelievable increase in my thigh mass. You can definitely expect big muscle gains when you use the power of the pyramid in your off-season workouts.

In order to avoid injuries, you should do all of your mass- and power-building exercises—regardless of how heavy the weight is—in strict form. The only exception to this rule is when you do one or two cheating reps (cheating is explained in detail later in this chapter) after a full set of strict reps taken to the point of momentary muscle failure.

At the competitive level of bodybuilding, there are two main causes of injuries: using poor form and trying a heavy exercise after you have rested too long and allowed your body to cool down. You can remove these causes of injuries simply by maintaining correct exercise form and not allowing your body to cool down between sets.

Basic vs. Isolation Exercises

In order to train productively in the off-season, you must understand the difference between *basic* and *isolation* exercises. You should also know the purpose of each type of movement. Every bodybuilding champion knows how to cycle basic and isolation exercises in his or her workout schedule to make the fastest gains in muscle mass.

Basic exercises work the large muscle groups of the body (such as the quadriceps, lats, pecs, traps, and spinal erectors) in concert with smaller muscle groups (such as the biceps, triceps, and deltoids). I do basic exercises with very heavy weights in strict form to build muscle mass and power. I use these movements far more in the off-season than during my precontest cycle. But even when honing muscles for a competition, I'll use one or two basic exercises for each muscle group in order to retain as much muscle mass as possible while dieting.

I'm from the old school of bodybuilders, and firmly believe in doing the basic movements and hoisting really big weights. It's actually difficult for me to get involved in doing a lot of little exercises without a lot of weight involved. I love to lift the most massive dumbbells I can find. When performing squats, it's great to hear the resounding clang of five or six 45-pound plates on each end of the bar as I do the movement.

In contrast to basic movements, isolation exercises work single muscle groups. Sometimes an isolation movement will stress just a part of a single muscle group. Generally speaking, isolation exercises are best for shaping a muscle group. They build very little mus-

cle mass. Since we're primarily concerned with building mass and power in the first third of this book, most of the exercises that I recommend in Chapter 4 are basic movements. When performed with maximum training poundages and in strict form, these basic exercises will enable you to make very fast gains in muscle mass and power.

To avoid confusion about basic and isolation exercises, refer to Figure 1–1 below, which lists the most commonly used movements for each muscle group.

Figure 1–1: Basic and Isolation Exercises

Muscle Group	Basic Exercises	Isolation Exercises
Thighs	Squats, Leg Presses, Stiff-legged Deadlifts	Leg Extensions and Curls
Trapezius	Barbell Upright Rows	Barbell and Dumbbell Shrugs
Latissimus Dorsi	Barbell, Dumbbell, and Pulley Rows; Chins, Lat-machine Pulldowns	Nautilus Pullovers, Barbell Bent-arm Pullovers
Erector Spinae	Deadlifts, Stiff-legged Deadlifts	Hyperextensions
Pectorals	Incline, Flat, and Decline Presses; Dips	Incline, Flat, and Decline Flyes; Pec-Deck Flyes
Deltoids	Barbell, Dumbbell, and Machine Overhead Presses; Upright Rows	Front Raises, Side Laterals, Bent Laterals
Biceps	Barbell and Dumbbell Curls; Preacher Curls	Barbell, Dumbbell, and Cable Concentration Curls
Triceps	Lying Barbell Triceps Extensions, Dips, Narrow-grip Bench Presses	Pulley Pushdowns, Dumbbell Kickbacks
Forearms	Barbell Reverse Curls	Barbell Wrist Curls
Calves	Seated and Standing Calf Machine Toe Raises	One-legged Calf Raises
Abdominals	Sit-ups, Leg Raises	Crunches

What back thickness! It takes plenty of 400-pound pulley rows and superheavy deadlifts to develop a back like Tom Platz's. (*Mike Neveux*)

Heavy vs. Light Training

You can conclude that I am an advocate of very heavy weight-training workouts. Undoubtedly, you will see "pumpers" in large gyms who lift very light weights with high reps and who have developed respectable physiques with such light training. However, such muscle tissue must be pumped up very regularly, or it inevitably and quickly deflates. Show me a pumper who's been on a one-month layoff from training, and I'll show you someone who has lost at least an inch from his or her upper arms.

Every bodybuilder loses a little muscle mass when he or she takes a layoff, but men and women who lift really heavy iron lose much less mass than pumpers. And heavy-training bodybuilders develop superior physiques with both great mass and outstanding muscularity.

Someone may have seen me training at Gold's Gym in Venice, California,

who'll say, "But I saw Tom Platz doing flat bench flyes with only a pair of 35-pound dumbbells!" Undoubtedly, I used them for one of my last sets of chest work following more than 20 continuous, all-out sets of pec training. They didn't see the 180-pound dumbbells I used for inclines and the 100-pounders I started my burnout series of flyes with before I gradually worked down to the 35s. And, believe me, at that point the 35s felt as if they weighed 200 pounds each because I don't rest between weight changes in this type of burnout series.

Split Routines

When you first started pumping iron, you probably followed a program in which you trained on three non-consecutive days per week, e.g., Mondays, Wednesdays, and Fridays. As long as you aren't doing too many sets for each muscle group, you'll make good progress on a three-day-per-week schedule. One way of increasing your workout intensity during the initial few months of training is to gradually add to the total number of sets you are doing for each muscle group. And it soon gets to the point where you don't have enough available energy to devote 100 percent intensity to every set in your lengthy routine. This is particularly true when you're expending a great deal of energy lifting the big iron.

Once you reach the point where you can't do justice to every muscle group in a full workout, you should begin using a split routine. Divide your body parts roughly into two halves, training the first half on Mondays and Thursdays, then bombing the second half on Tuesdays and Fridays. This plan allows each body part plenty of time to recuperate between workouts. And since each training session is shorter than in a complete workout plan, you can work every muscle group with maximum mental and physical energy, which guarantees that you will make great muscle gains.

The following are two alternate ways in which you can divide up your body parts for a four-day split routine (note that calves and abdominals can be trained each workout day).

Alternative 1

Monday-Thursday	Tuesday-Friday
Abdominals	Abdominals
Chest	Thighs
Shoulders	Upper Arms
Back	Forearms
Calves	Calves

Alternative 2

Monday-Thursday	Tuesday-Friday
Abdominals	Abdominals
Chest	Back
Thighs	Shoulders
Biceps	Triceps
Forearms	Neck
Calves	Calves

Unless you have been working out steadily for at least two years, you probably won't make acceptable gains training more than four days per week. However, at about the two-year point (the precise timing depends on how quickly your body builds up its recuperative ability), you can switch to a five-day split routine in which you train Monday through Friday and rest on the weekend.

When you follow a five-day split routine, you divide your body parts into two groups, just as for a four-day split. For the sake of clarity, let's label the Monday-Thursday portion of either four-day split that I've presented as "A" and the Tuesday-Friday portion as "B." The first week that you follow a five-day split, do part A on Monday, Wednesday, and Friday, part B on Tuesday and Thursday. During the second week, you do part B on Monday, Wednesday, and Friday, part A on Tuesday and Thursday. Week three repeats week one, week four repeats week two, and so on, ad infinitum.

Just so there is no confusion about how a five-day split routine works, the following is a program of five weeks.

	Mon	Tues	Wed	Thurs	Fri
Week 1	A	B	A	B	A
Week 2	B	A	B	A	B
Week 3	A	B	A	B	A
Week 4	B	A	B	A	B
Week 5	A	B	A	B	A

Virtually all bodybuilders train six days per week prior to a competition, and a few are even able to make good gains training six days per week in the off-season. However, I don't recommend working major muscle groups three days per week on a six-day split in the off-season. You will make much more positive progress with two workouts for each major body part on a six-day-per-week off-season split routine.

The following is one of several ways in which you can divide up your body parts for a six-day off-season split routine.

Monday-Thursday	Tuesday-Friday	Wednesday-Saturday
Abdominals	Abdominals	Abdominals
Chest	Back	Thighs
Shoulders	Upper Arms	Calves
Neck	Forearms	Forearms

As you experiment with a six-day split routine, you may find that you can't recuperate sufficiently between workouts to do justice to your next training session. This is a good indication that you should drop back to five- or even four-day-per-week training.

Everything I write in this book is a *suggestion* of what I feel might work for you, and which you should give a trial to in your own workouts. It may or may not work for you. I give training seminars all over America, Canada, and the rest of the world, and bodybuilders everywhere want to know *exactly* what will work for them. Unfortunately, I can't give definitive answers because every person's body is uniquely different from everyone else's. So, in reality, one of the biggest secrets of bodybuilding success is that you have to learn for yourself what works best for you.

The Four-Day Workout Cycle

If six-day-per-week training is a little too much for your body to handle, you might profit from following a four-day cycle in which you work out three days and then rest on the fourth day before repeating the cycle. This is very similar to the five-day training cycle that I follow, which was described earlier in this chapter.

The following is an example of how you can divide up your body parts for a four-day training cycle.

Day 1	Day 2	Day 3
Abdominals	Abdominals	Abdominals
Chest	Thighs	Shoulders
Upper Back	Lower Back	Upper Arms
Calves	Forearms	Calves

Day 4   Rest

The famous Tom Platz thighs under tension on a leg-extension machine. (Craig Dietz)

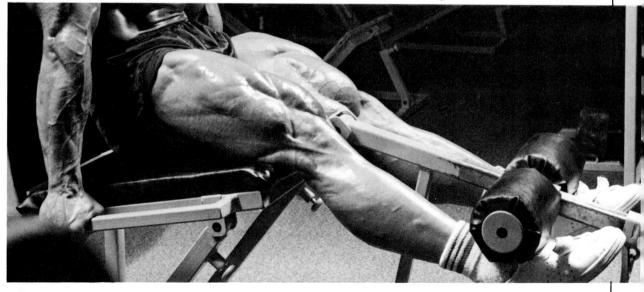

There are many contemporary bodybuilding champions who follow a four-day training cycle, and its popularity is increasing each passing month. Perhaps it will work as well for you.

Free Weights vs. Machines

Many gym equipment manufacturers tout their machines as the last word in training equipment. In my opinion, there are advantages to both machine and free-weight training in bodybuilding. There are a lot of ways in which you can put resistance on a muscle. For your chest you can do push-ups, bench presses with a barbell or two dumbbells, or you can do bench presses on a variety of machines, such as Nautilus, Corbin-Pacific, Brother, Universal, and many others. I don't feel any difference in the quality of stress placed on my pecs by a machine versus the stress I can place on my chest muscles doing barbell or dumbbell bench presses.

The main advantage of exercise machines is that—unlike free weights—they offer direct, rotary, balanced resistance throughout the full range of movement in each exercise. Also, machines normally have built-in safety factors. But on the opposite side of the coin, there's very little variety in the number of movements that you can do with machines in comparison to free-weight exercises. To keep your muscles growing, you need to shock them, and this requires changes in the exercises that you do for each muscle group.

Training Programs

I don't have any strict rule about how frequently I change to a new training program. Before a competition, however, I always stick with my favorite exercises and routines. That's not a good time to take chances experimenting with new exercises, routines, or training techniques. However, during the off-season, I'll experiment to expand myself as a bodybuilder, and I'll change my programs around quite frequently.

There are many schools of thought on how often you should switch to a new training program. Most experts recommend switching to a new routine each four to six weeks. However, Arnold Schwarzenegger believes that a bodybuilder should stick to the same program once he or she has found one that works well. And hulking Lou Ferrigno prefers to do a new training routine each time he works out.

Your basic temperament will dictate how frequently you should switch to a new training program. You can begin by switching to a new routine every month, then experiment with changing programs more or less frequently. If you are a stoic, plodding type of person, you will no doubt thrive on following a routine for many months at a time. And if you are a more excitable and easily bored individual, you will probably make your best progress switching to a new training schedule every time you go into the gym.

Hard Gainers

Thousands of young bodybuilders who are making slow progress from their training cop out and console themselves by believing they are "hard gainers" who will never build enough quality muscle tissue to win a bodybuilding championship. Well, if that is the case, I'm a hard gainer, too. I think that everyone is a hard gainer because it's simply not easy to gain muscle mass. You have to fight for every ounce of new muscle, and everyone can make gains if he or she is dedicated and consistent in his or her training.

Former Mr. America Roger Callard (left) is suitably impressed by Tom's fantastic leg development just prior to the 1977 Mr. America show where Platz was second in his class. (Art Zeller)

Naturally, the rate at which different people make bodybuilding gains varies widely. If you looked at an early photograph of Lou Ferrigno, who was 5 feet 10 inches tall and weighed only 130 pounds when he started working out, you'd never have been able to predict that he'd become a great bodybuilding star. But 10 years later he had grown to 6 feet 5 inches and weighed a very muscular 265 pounds. He won the Mr. America, Mr. Universe (twice), and Mr. International titles, and would probably also have become Mr. Olympia if he hadn't turned to acting. Every ounce of the 135 pounds that Lou put on over the years came only with great difficulty.

One common problem with hard gainers is that they're chronically overtrained. They try to follow the training programs of their favorite champion as they appear in *Muscle & Fitness* or some other bodybuilding magazine, and the routine is much too intense for them to handle. As a result, they overtrain and don't make any gains.

Even when doing a relatively light exercise such as cross-bench pullovers, Tom Platz takes it to the limit. (*Mike Neveux*)

In the minds of many people, more is supposed to be better, but in bodybuilding I personally feel that less is more productive as long as the shorter workouts are of greater intensity. I know top bodybuilders who work out five to eight hours per day, but they can only do so when they have a very low level of training intensity in their workouts. I personally train very hard, and it would kill me if I had to work out more than two hours per day. To me, the idea of going into a gym knowing I'd have to be there for five hours would be the worst possible form of torture.

If you are taking short, intense workouts and are totally into your bodybuilding, but you are still not making any gains, take a close look at your diet. Larry Scott, the first Mr. Olympia winner, was a self-confessed hard gainer, and he believed that the optimum bodybuilding diet he followed was responsible for at least 75 percent of his success at build-ing massive muscles. I believe that nutrition is important, but certainly not more important than a correct mental approach to bodybuilding. However, I believe that in the long run diet is more important than training.

Training to Failure

To receive the most benefit from conventional bodybuilding training, you should push each post-warm-up set to the point of "failure." There are several definitions of training to failure, but I define it as continuing a set of any exercise in strict form to the point where you can no longer complete a repetition. For example, when performing standing barbell curls, you do seven strict reps, but can only curl the bar on the eighth rep about a third of the way up before it stalls out. (In Chapter 5, I'll explain my concept of going to total muscle failure in much greater detail.)

I've noticed that a lot of aspiring bodybuilders avoid taking each set to failure, which robs them of much of the musclebuilding benefit of the set. A normal excuse for this is that it hurts to train so hard. Of course it hurts, but in bodybuilding a popular maxim is, "No pain, no gain." Another rationalization is that pushing every set to failure will lead to overtraining. If you do six-hour workouts pushing every set to failure, you *will* overtrain, but a one- or two-hour session with most sets to failure just builds muscle, and it builds it very quickly.

After a six-week break-in of training to failure, you will begin to train *past* the point of failure on some of your sets, which will induce an even faster rate of muscle growth. I train past failure on virtually every set once I'm fully warmed up, and I'd never have achieved my current degree of muscle mass if I hadn't trained like this the past few years.

The two best methods of pushing a set past the point of normal momentary muscular failure are *cheating* and *forced reps*.

Cheating

Beginning weight trainees are invariably cautioned against cheating in an exercise because they invariably use extraneous body movement to make a set easier to do. They swing their bodies or jerk their legs to make the bar go up more easily. On the other hand, I cheat to add intensity to a muscle, rather than to remove stress from it. And that's the secret to cheating that all top bodybuilders use to force a muscle to continue working long past the point of normal failure.

Let's use barbell curls as an example of how to correctly use the cheating method. Load up a barbell with a weight that you can curl for six or seven reps in strict form. Pick up the weight and do a

When working his deltoids to the max, Tom often spreads his legs to force out even more presses behind neck. He'll cheat with his legs in order to get the weight up one more time. (*Mike Neveux*)

If incline sit-ups become impossible to complete under normal abdominal power, Platz grasps the sides of the abdominal board and gives himself just enough of a forced rep to grind out a few more. (*Mike Neveux*)

set of barbell curls to the point of failure, but don't then put the bar down as so many other bodybuilders do. Once you fail to finish a rep, you should use just enough body swing to add sufficient momentum to the bar to swing it past the sticking point at which it stalled out. It's essential that you don't impart even an ounce more momentum to the bar than is needed to cheat up the rep. Then you should lower the weight as slowly as possible, resisting its downward momentum with all of your strength.

When you do cheating reps, your muscles will grow fatigued so quickly that you need not do more than two or three of them. Past two or three cheating reps, your biceps will be growing so fatigued that it is of little or no value to do additional ones.

Forced Reps

Forced reps are a more precise way of removing just enough weight from a bar to allow yourself to complete a rep past the point of failure. Let's say you are doing a set of bench presses with 225 pounds and fail to complete your sixth repetition. Failing with that rep merely means that you can't press out 225, but you can probably do a rep with 215 pounds, and perhaps even a second one with 200 pounds.

With forced reps, your training partner will lift the bar up just enough to remove the weight that keeps you from completing a repetition on your own. He literally allows you to force out two or three reps past the point of failure. And as with cheating reps, more than two or three forced reps won't give you additional benefit.

I use both cheating and forced reps in my off-season workouts, and get a lot out of pushing my muscles past the normal point of failure in each exercise. I am totally convinced that you will greatly increase your bodybuilding gains by using cheating reps and forced reps. However, I don't think that cheating, forced reps, and other advanced techniques should be attempted by bodybuilders who have not already mastered the aspects of basic training.

Supersets

Supersets are combinations of two exercises performed with minimal rest between movements followed by a normal rest interval of approximately 60 seconds. Supersets are a significant step up the ladder of training intensity from straight sets, so it's necessary to work slowly into using them. Otherwise, you will overstress yourself and won't be able to complete the remainder of your training session.

The most fundamental type of superset includes exercises for antagonistic muscle groups, such as the biceps and triceps, pecs and lats, quadriceps and hamstrings, and other groupings. The following are typical examples of supersets for antagonistic muscle groups.

Biceps + Triceps = Barbell Curls
　　+ Pulley Pushdowns
Forearm Flexors + Forearm
　　Extensors = Barbell Wrist
　　Curls + Barbell Reverse Wrist
　　Curls
Pecs + Lats = Bench Presses + Lat
　　Machine Pulldowns
Quads + Hamstrings = Leg
　　Extensions + Leg Curls

A much more intense form of superset involves performing two consecutive exercises for the same muscle group, taking no rest between movements, but taking a normal rest interval between supersets. The following are typical examples of supersets for single muscle groups.

Quadriceps = Leg Presses + Leg
    Extensions
Hamstrings = Leg Curls + Stiff-
    legged Deadlifts
Calves = Seated Calf Raises +
    Standing Calf Raises
Traps = Upright Rows + Shrugs
Lats = Bent-arm Pullovers +
    Seated Pulley Rowing
Deltoids = Presses Behind Neck +
    Side Laterals
Pecs = Bench Presses + Flat-bench
    Flyes
Biceps = Barbell Preacher Curls +
    Standing Preacher Curls
Triceps = Lying Triceps Extensions
    + Close-grip Bench Presses

Power-Rack Training

Some of today's strongest and most massive bodybuilders occasionally do partial, superheavy movements in a power rack. I personally don't do much work on a power rack, although it can be of benefit to some bodybuilders who want to increase their strength. I did a lot more power-rack training when I was powerlifting, which I think is more conducive to building great strength than developing larger muscles.

Instead of doing partial movements in a power rack to develop greater tendon and ligament strength, I prefer to do full movements until I reach the point where I can no longer finish a rep. Then I either do cheating reps, forced reps, or a type of partial rep called "burns," which is discussed in Chapter 5. And sometimes when I can no longer even move the weight an inch, I will hold it as long as I can while tensing and stretching the working muscles.

Overtraining

Essentially, this is a condition in which you chronically train so much that your body is unable to recuperate between workouts. You develop a greater and greater recuperation debt, until finally your body becomes overtrained, often breaking down and becoming ill.

The following is a list of the ten most common symptoms of overtraining.

- Persistent lack of pep and energy
- Lack of enthusiasm for workouts
- Persistently sore joints and/or muscles
- Loss of appetite
- Insomnia
- Elevated morning pulse rate
- Elevated morning blood pressure
- Irritability
- Deterioration of neuro-muscular coordination
- Injury and/or illness

The best remedy for overtraining is to avoid it in the first place. Generally speaking, it is caused by very long workouts. If you train very intensely and as I recommend, you probably won't overtrain.

A second overtraining prevention measure is to take periodic, short layoffs from training. One or two weeks off each four to six months will do wonders in elevating your enthusiasm for training. Even just taking an extra day of rest between workouts when you are feeling overly fatigued will help to prevent an overtrained condition. I personally never work out when I am feeling too fatigued to be enthusiastic about getting into the gym and banging around the iron.

If you exhibit two or more of the above symptoms of an overtrained state, you must take steps to eliminate the overtrained condition. The first step is to take a one- or two-week layoff from training. And when you do get back into the gym, you should be careful to switch to a new training program which features far fewer sets for each body part and much greater intensity within each set. Then you'll be back on track building muscle mass at a normal rate of speed.

The Tom Platz Extended-Sets Training System

Although I independently developed my own system of training, I ultimately discovered that it is a combination of the systems of Arnold Schwarzenegger and Mike Mentzer. I agree with many of the features of each of these champion's training techniques, but not completely.

Mike Mentzer's concept of anaerobic training in the gym and aerobic training outside of the gym, as well as his preference of training past the point of failure, makes good sense to me. But I can't agree with doing as few total sets as he does. In that respect, I'm more in line with Arnold Schwarzenegger, who believes that you need to perform plenty of total sets in order to develop maximum muscular detail.

I firmly believe that you have the right to make up your own mind about how you will train, just as I did when I was a bit younger. I suggest that you make an in-depth study of every top bodybuilder's training system, then utilize those parts of each system that work best for your unique body. I feel that my own extended-sets system would put muscle on a skeleton, but I don't have such a big ego that I would say it will work for everyone.

Ultimately, you will probably take parts of my extended-sets system that work well for you, then perhaps incorporate some advice from Arnold, something from Franco Columbu, a bit from Frank Zane, and so on, until you have

The incredibly high intensity of Tom's extended-sets training principle is evident as he nears the end of an all-out set of seated pulley rows. (John Balik)

developed your own unique system. Unfortunately, I can't feel out each exercise, routine, and training technique for you, but you'll soon learn to do this quite well for yourself. And in the end, you'll adapt my extended-sets system of training to suit your own unique needs.

2 Off-Season Diet

It's very important that you be aware of your food consumption on a year-round basis. As long as your mind is properly keyed in, diet and training are equally vital considerations during an off-season cycle. And prior to a competition, your degree of success can be attributed to nutrition by as much as 70–80 percent.

I'd like to tell you *exactly* what to eat during an off-season training cycle, but you must understand that there are no absolutes in bodybuilding. All I can do is tell you what *should* work and let you experiment with each variable for yourself.

Weight-Gain Diet

It's relatively easy for most people to gain body fat, but the key is to attempt to gain as much muscle as possible. Inevitably, you will also gain a little fat during the off-season, but the emphasis should be on gaining muscle mass.

Your protein consumption — type, amount, and timing—is crucial in a weight-gaining diet because protein makes up the muscle tissue in your body. If you can increase the amount of high-quality protein that your body digests and transfers into your bloodstream, you have a much greater chance of assimilating that protein into muscle tissue.

Protein

The protein in human muscle cells is made up of 22 basic components called *amino acids*. Of these 22 amino acids, 14 can be manufactured within your body just from the foods you normally consume each day, regardless of what they are. There are eight additional ones, termed *essential amino acids*, that must be present in the protein foods you consume for your body to utilize supplies of the other 14 aminos that it manufactures.

Protein with all eight essential amino acids present in good supply is termed *complete protein*, and it's the best quality of protein for use in gaining weight. All animal-source proteins— meat, fish, poultry, milk products, eggs— are complete protein. On the other hand, most vegetable-source proteins are *incomplete proteins*, lacking in one or more of the essential amino acids.

Among vegetable proteins, the most complete are soybeans and sprouted seeds, but they are still inferior to complete proteins. However, by combining these lesser-quality protein foods from vegetarian sources with complete protein (e.g., combining corn with cheese), you can greatly augment the quality of vegetable-source proteins.

Nutritionists have come up with a protein efficiency ratio (PER) to rate the quality of each protein food, or the ease with which it can be assimilated by your body into muscle and other body tissues. The highest PER belongs to egg whites, followed by fish meal and milk. Poultry and red meats are ranked somewhat lower, but certainly not as low as the vegetable-source proteins.

The bottom line is this: You must consume foods with high PERs if you want to gain muscle mass. Train as hard as you want to, but be sure to eat ample quantities of fish, eggs, milk, poultry, and red meat.

The amount of protein you consume at each meal is also vitally important. Depending on your bodyweight (actually, on the size of your stomach) and relative digestive efficiency, your body can digest and make ready for assimilation into muscle tissue 20–30 grams of protein each meal. Excessive amounts of it can clog up your digestive system and make it less efficient. You have to eat at least enough protein for your body to digest its maximum level of the food, but not so much that you impede the digestive process.

You should eat 20–30 grams of complete protein each time you sit down to a meal. If you are smaller of build, eat something close to the lowest of these two figures; if you are larger, eat up to 30 grams per meal. And if you are taking a digestive support (which is discussed a bit later in this chapter), you can also eat a bit more protein, perhaps five grams more than normal each meal.

Figure 2–1: Suggested Weight-Gain Menu

Meal 1 (8:00 A.M.). Cheese omelette, 2 slices whole-grain bread, milk, supplements.
Meal 2 (10:30 A.M.). Tuna salad, 2 slices whole-grain bread, slice of hard cheese, fruit juice.
Meal 3 (1:00 P.M.). Broiled chicken, rice, small salad, iced tea, supplements.
Meal 4 (3:30 P.M.). Protein drink, supplements.
Meal 5 (6:00 P.M.). Broiled steak, baked potato, green vegetable, milk, supplements.
Meal 6 (8:30 P.M.). Cold cuts, 2 slices whole-grain bread, yogurt, raw nuts and seeds, glass of milk.

The Food and Drug Administration recommends approximately one-half gram of protein per pound of body weight for basic tissue maintenance. For active athletes, I feel that between three-quarters and one gram of protein per pound of bodyweight is more appropri-

ate. Therefore, a 180-pound man should consume between 135 and 180 grams of first-class protein per day.

You may have already calculated that a 180-pound man eating 30 grams of protein three times per day will consume only 90 grams, a figure well short of the 135–180 range. The answer to this knotty problem is to eat more than three meals per day, but to keep them small and made up of adequate amounts of complete protein foods. Rather than the traditional two or three large meals per day, bodybuilders interested in gaining weight will eat four to six times each day. And, the 180-pound man who consumes 30 grams of protein each meal will end up consuming 180 grams per day if he can eat six times.

These small, frequent meals should be evenly spaced out during the day, allowing for no more than three hours to elapse between feedings. A suggested weight-gain menu is presented in Figure 2–1 on this page. Take a good look at it, and feel free to adapt it to include the foods that you prefer to eat, just as long as you also stay within the other guidelines presented in this section.

Digestive Supports

Another way in which to increase the amount of protein digested at each meal is to take digestive enzymes every time you eat. There are special enzymes that help you to digest fats and carbohydrates as well as proteins. I take three different tablets each meal in order to help digest these three major food elements.

You can purchase a wide variety of digestive enzymes at health-food stores. You can even buy hydrochloric acid tablets, although I've never used them myself, to facilitate protein digestion. Simply read each bottle that you find in the digestive-supports section of the store, noting what each preparation will help you digest and the relative cost of each, and buy the product that will best benefit your body.

Milk and Weight Gain

Milk, with its combination of protein, fats, and carbohydrates, is still one of the best foods for gaining weight. Unfortunately, many individuals suffer from lactose intolerance, which is an allergy to lactose, the sugar found in milk. As a result, they cannot comfortably drink milk.

Symptoms of lactose intolerance are stomach bloating, drowsiness, lassitude, and general malaise. However, you can avoid lactose intolerance by taking lactase tablets (lactase is the enzyme that digests lactose), which are available over the counter at most pharmacies. One or two tablets taken with a glass of milk allow your body to safely and comfortably digest the lactose.

Another way to consume milk products and avoid lactose intolerance is to consume hard cheeses and/or yogurt, each of which has had the lactose removed when the milk was processed.

If you can drink milk—or have otherwise solved a lactose intolerance problem—it's best to consume certified raw milk and milk products, which you can find in many supermarkets and most health-food stores. Raw milk is free from harmful bacteria and has not had its nutrients denatured by the heating process used in pasteurization.

If there is a lack of fat in my diet, I will not gain weight even when I'm consuming a high number of calories. As a result, I must resort to eating concentrated, high-fat calories, such as found in milk. I used to drink a half gallon of whole milk after every workout, and I made great gains in muscle mass as a result.

My theory is that when you keep fat intake low all year long, you lose the enzymes in your stomach needed to digest and burn fat. So I'll eat plenty of fat in the off-season and then follow a low-fat/low-calorie diet during a peaking cycle.

Younger guys really burn up calories just in growing and reaching maturity. Therefore, they have to eat even more calories than normal in order to gain weight, and it's easier to drink calories than to eat them. For these two reasons, milk is an ideal food source. Many of the best bodybuilders—myself included—have consistently consumed a gallon or more of milk each day for many years.

Protein Supplements

Supplemental proteins are an essential part of the weight-gaining diet, as long as they are from animal sources, such as milk and eggs, rather than soybean flour. It's particularly good to take a protein supplement when you are a little rushed and might otherwise have missed a scheduled meal. It only takes a couple of minutes to whip up a protein shake in a blender and drink it, and the shake is a superior source of muscle-building protein.

The following is an easy recipe for a protein shake:

    8–10 oz. milk
    1 rounded tbs. protein powder
    3–4 strawberries (or other soft fruit
        for flavoring)

Mix this concoction in a blender for about a minute, adding a little shaved ice if your milk is not already cold.

Vitamins

No one who is unhealthy can hope to make good gains in muscle mass. Therefore, you must take food supplements that will help you to remain healthy. The best way to ensure that you are receiving sufficient quantities of vitamins, minerals, and trace elements is to take one or two multipacks of these supplements per day. And it's always best for you to take vitamins and minerals with a meal; they aren't absorbed as efficiently when not taken with food.

Vitamin B complex is also an important weight-gaining supplement, because the B vitamins are useful in stimulating a healthy appetite and in tissue formation. One high-potency capsule per meal would be a minimum recommended consumption when in a mass-building cycle. B complex is water soluble and regularly flushes from your body in your urine. Therefore, it must be taken frequently each day.

Tom Platz's Off-Season Diet

During the off-season, I purposely increase my intake of high-fat, red meats. Otherwise, I simply follow a well-balanced diet. I keep a low level of vitamin and mineral intake during the off-season, which allows me to obtain a greater response from the supplements once I start taking them prior to a competition. I'll take a multipack, or just a one-a-day multiple vitamin and mineral tablet. Sometimes I don't take any supplements at all. When I'm eating well I don't need that many supplements.

Most bodybuilders are hung up on what I call a "more is better" syndrome. They feel that if 10 sets is getting the job done, 20 would be twice as good. Well, more isn't necessarily better, either in

Tom's last day of training prior to the 1980 Mr. Olympia competition in Sydney, Australia, was filmed for a local production entitled "The Comeback," a reference to Arnold Schwarzenegger's return to competition. (*John Balik*)

training or diet. In terms of supplementation during an off-season cycle, less is better.

I write down everything I eat in a diary, carefully monitoring my caloric intake every day, as well as noting the types of foods I'm eating. In this way, I am able to tell that I simply can't get cross striations in my major muscle groups without going on a low-fat/low-calorie diet. I can lose a lot of body fat on a low-carbohydrate regimen, but simply can't get the type of striations it takes to win an Olympia.

I've also noticed that the number of calories I take in and their effect on my body are both relative. They depend totally on my mental attitude. I could be eating half of the world every day, and I wouldn't make weight gains if my mind wasn't into it. By thinking big, I get big.

Let me give you an example. After the 1980 Mr. Universe show, at which I weighed 193, I went home and started a weight-gaining binge. I was eating 6000 calories per day! I wouldn't go to bed each night until I *had* eaten all 6000 calories, right down to the last pint of ice cream. But I made the mistake of not being mentally into the process, and I didn't gain an ounce until I started lying in bed each night visualizing myself getting bigger.

My mass-building maxim is: *Think mass, eat mass, train mass.* I'd even suggest that you print up a sign with this maxim and place it over your posting mirror so you'll be constantly reminded of its importance.

I'm sure you'd like to know precisely how I eat to gain additional muscle mass during an off-season cycle. The following is a typical daily menu for off-season eating.

Morning (prior to training). Two pieces of whole-grain toast with butter and jelly; juice or milk; coffee; supplements (if actually taking any that day).

Lunch (after my workout). Three to six eggs (sunny side up); hamburger patty; sliced tomatoes; juice (something like grapefruit or tomato); two pieces of bread or a bran muffin.

Snack. Cheese (quite a bit) and crackers, a glass of milk or more juice.

Dinner. A very large piece of prime rib; salad (with cottage cheese, nuts, and everything else you'd find in a good salad bar); bread and butter; sometimes a potato; a piece of pie or ice cream; coffee or milk.

Late Evening Snack. A couple of pints of ice cream or a bag of nuts.

I definitely believe in eating late in the evening when on a weight-gaining program. The food seems to be assimilated much more easily late at night than earlier in the day. You might have a lower metabolism than I do and consequently won't be able to get away with eating the ice cream, but you can certainly consume protein foods prior to hopping into bed.

You can see from the information in this chapter that I don't go overboard in adopting elaborate eating practices. I don't eat raw glandular supplements; I don't eat a ton of amino acid capsules (they tend to bloat me); and I don't notice any added energy from taking 100 desiccated liver tablets per day.

There's so much total bunk written and said about the process of attaining a winning physique that I simply can't believe it sometimes. What really works is the basics—hard, heavy training; a healthy, balanced, high-calorie diet; and a positive mental approach to bodybuilding. This is definitely a no-frills approach to the sport, but it's also a winning approach. Give it a try!

3 Training Factors for the Off-Season

You should have two main objectives during an off-season training cycle—to generally increase your muscle mass and, more particularly, to improve weak body parts. During a precontest cycle, you'll be so busy just stripping away all superfluous body fat that it will be impossible to improve a lagging muscle group. And a precontest cycle will last only a couple of months, too little time to make meaningful improvements in either all-around muscle mass or the mass and quality of a weak body part.

In this chapter, I will discuss the following important off-season training factors: how to smash past sticking points; training partners; weightlifting belts and body wraps; individualized routines; variable routines; layoffs; stress management; flexibility training; stretch marks; supination in biceps training; and how to cope with injuries.

Sticking Points

Sticking points in your progress are inevitable in bodybuilding. For many months, perhaps even years, you cruise along making great gains from your training, then suddenly you stop dead in your tracks. Despite your best efforts in the gym, you are no longer able to make noticeable progress. You have reached a sticking point.

I define a sticking point as not making any gains for a couple of months. The way you feel—constantly fatigued, your muscles flaccid, the weights no longer increasing, lack of a muscle pump—can also define a sticking point for you.

There are both mental and physical causes for a sticking point, but most often one is caused by deep fatigue. Let me give you an example. When I was younger, I spent several months bench-pressing just under 300 pounds. Try as I might, I simply couldn't get past the 300 barrier. Then I was forced to take a week off training for final exams in school. When I got back into the gym, I was able to bench-press 300 pounds for reps. I had been overtraining and simply not giving myself enough time to fully recuperate between workouts.

If mental boredom is the problem, you can vault past a sticking point in your progress simply by changing to a new training program, or by moving over to a different gym for a few workouts. But if the problem is overtraining and incomplete recuperation, you must take a more complicated course to solve your sticking point.

To smash past a physical sticking point, I suggest first taking a one-week layoff (discussed later in this chapter) from training to allow your body and mind to completely recuperate. I also feel that it's a good idea to increase your caloric intake while you are away from the gym.

After returning to the gym, you should initially try cutting back on both the number of days you are training each week and the total number of sets you perform for each muscle group. If you are on a six-day split routine, for example, you can try a four-day training cycle, three days of training followed by a rest day. Or you can drop back to only four workouts per week.

At the same time that you decrease the total number of sets performed for each body part by about 20 percent, you should correspondingly increase the actual training intensity within each set. You'll never overtrain by working out too

Look at the striations in Tom's lower lats as he does pulldowns behind neck. (*Mike Neveux*)

I *must* do my own workouts. Unless a training partner does exactly what I do—he gives me more than I give him—I can't work out with him. But people don't like to sacrifice their own training for you. I'm very selfish about my training needs, and I'm not afraid to admit it. As a pro bodybuilder, my training *must* be at an optimum level at all times.

On the other hand, there are many bodybuilders who simply can't push themselves hard enough on their own, and they must have a training partner. I see many bodybuilders like this, and there's nothing wrong with it as long as they feel it's an even trade-off to sacrifice

Tom flexes for his buddies in the gym. (*Mike Neveux*)

hard, only by doing too lengthy workouts. And, as I've noted, more sticking points are caused by overtraining than by any other factor.

Training Partners

Whether or not you choose to use a training partner is a totally personal decision. I very seldom have an actual training partner. Instead, I train alone and rely on others in the gym to hand me heavy dumbbells and spot me for heavy lifts like maxed-out squats. And, in turn, I'll help them in their workouts.

a little in their workouts to gain the assistance of a training partner.

Belts and Wraps

The more consistently heavy you train, the more likely you will need the support provided by a weightlifting belt and joint wraps. I wear a weightlifting belt for all heavy movements, particularly for squats, back exercises, and overhead lifts. I like feeling the tightness around my waist when I'm pumping heavy iron, and I feel that my lower back needs to be braced for the heavier lifts. You're inherently unstable through your midsection, so the bracing of the belt is valuable.

Using a weightlifting belt is a carry-over from my powerlifting days. No one is going to try a 700-pound squat without wearing a weightlifting belt. You'd probably break your back if you tried it. So it's far more comfortable for me to use a belt when I'm doing squats and other maxed-out exercises.

If you don't already have one, a weightlifting belt will cost between $30 (for the most stripped-down model) to over $60 (for a custom-made belt). Weightlifting belts are available at many sporting goods stores, as well as through mail-order ads in magazines.

I never use joint wraps during a workout. A few years ago I developed a knee problem from long periods of sitting during plane flights. For a short time, I used knee wraps, but I noticed that there was less stress on my thighs and more on my butt and lower back when I did squats using wraps. As a result, I decided to never again use joint wraps. Wraps make your legs and other limbs into levers, rather than letting them bear the stress of each exercise. Avoid wraps, and I'm sure that you'll end up with better development in the long run.

Individualized Routines

There are a sufficient number of training routines presented in this book to keep you going for at least a couple of years. But sooner or later you will have to start making up your own training programs. With the suggestions given in this section, however, you will have little difficulty in formulating your own routines in the future.

First and foremost, you must always train every muscle group (with the exception of your neck, which will grow in mass just from the exercises you perform for peripheral muscle groups, such as the shoulders, upper back and upper chest). This will keep your body proportions even, as long as you always place priority on your weak muscle groups. Lagging body parts should be trained as hard as possible early in your workouts when you have maximum mental and physical energy to devote to all-out workouts.

It's also essential that you always train your arms after your torso muscle groups. Your arm muscles are involved in basic exercises for your torso (e.g., your triceps are directly involved in bench presses for your pectorals). And since your arm muscles are smaller and weaker than your torso groups, they normally fatigue and give out before you have pushed your pecs, lats, traps, and delts to the limit. Further weakening your biceps and triceps with direct training before hitting your torso muscle groups aggravates this problem.

Because overtraining is such a chronic problem among aspiring bodybuilders, I feel that the number of sets you perform for each muscle group is crucial. Taking into consideration the fact that individuals have varying degrees of recuperative ability, I feel that intermediate bodybuilders with less than one year of steady training can best profit from 8–10 total sets for each large muscle group (thighs, back, chest) and five to seven total sets for smaller body parts. For advanced bodybuilders, 12–15 sets would be appropriate for large muscle groups and 8–10 sets for smaller body parts.

Of course, the above figures go out the window when you enter a precontest cycle. Then most bodybuilders do drastically more total sets for each muscle group. Keep in mind that there is an overlap between body parts, and you will achieve the best muscle tie-ins if you do primarily basic exercises. For example, when you're training your chest with benches, inclines, and dips, you can't help also stressing your anterior/medial delts and triceps.

Finally, there are no definite rules in bodybuilding. You must constantly experiment on your body in order to determine exactly how each external stimulus affects your unique physique. Therefore, you may be at odds with some things I suggest, both in terms of making up your own routines and general bodybuilding practices. Go with your own instincts; you're much more of an expert about your own body than I could ever hope to be.

Variable Routines

If you do the same training programs over and over for weeks and months at a time, your mind and body will eventually become so used to the training that your muscles will fail to continue responding to the exercise stimuli. My body definitely gets used to the same programs, so I am careful to change something every workout. I have a set routine, but I am constantly changing the stimuli. For example, I'll vary the angle of an incline bench, train some body parts on dif- ferent days, or do a higher or lower number of reps each set. I'll even substitute different (but equivalent) exercises for a particular muscle group.

In short, I am constantly changing the intensity of my workouts in ways other than varying the amount of weight I use. This keeps my muscles off-balance, and they are not able to adapt to a particular type of stress. As a result, my muscles are constantly forced to grow in mass and power.

Layoffs

I suggest taking a layoff of one week every three to four months. I take a week off three or four times per year according to my exhibition schedule and how my body feels at the time. If I have some time off from exhibitions and I'm feeling depleted, I won't hesitate to take a one-week layoff. Layoffs help you to recuperate your energy supplies and allow you to heal up the minor injuries that you inevitably receive in a heavy training cycle.

I prefer an active type of layoff in which I avoid the gym while still staying physically active riding my bike, playing tennis, and so forth. If I'm really burned out, however, I may just lie around my apartment. When you have severely depleted your energy reserves, it's foolish to force yourself to work out. Use your training instinct to decide whether a layoff should be active or passive.

Stress Management

Stress can be both positive and negative. The late Dr. Hans Selye, the world's foremost stress researcher, named negative stress *distress* and positive stress *eustress*. And he pointed out that both types of stress evoke similar physiological responses—elevated pulse rate and blood

During a layoff from the weights, Tom does some aerobic exercise such as riding a bicycle.
(*Mike Neveux*)

pressure, a release of adrenaline into the blood stream, and heightened sensory perception. Distress can have a harmful long-range effect on the human body, while eustress is beneficial.

Let me give you examples of distress and eustress. You feel distress if you have been sitting in a car fighting rush-hour traffic. And eustress is the exhilarated feeling you might get from sky diving or hang gliding.

I function and respond best under heavy stress. When I'm travelling around Europe giving exhibitions every night, I tend to train well and get into my best shape. But when I have no pressing need to be in top shape, it's difficult for me to train truly hard and reach peak condition. I use potentially negative stress in a positive manner to motivate myself to excel.

The correct method of bodybuilding can help to control negative stress. However, there are far too many young guys who let training rule their lives. Don't become obsessive and put harmful stress on yourself.

Flexibility Training

Regular stretching is an important part of my overall training philosophy. I stretch every morning both before and after I train. Sometimes I'll even stretch in the middle of a workout. My program only lasts about fifteen minutes, but it produces a very beneficial effect on my physique.

Stretching is an excellent warm-up and cool-down activity for your joints and muscles. If you have greater flexibility, you can use the weights over a longer range of movement, which helps to prevent injuries and develop a better quality of physique.

I also find it important to stretch each muscle and its tendons before the muscle is fully contracted. This practice helps to compensate for the Golgi tendon reflex, which overprotects your tendons from injury by limiting contractions. In other words, you'll get a much more complete contraction if you first elongate the muscle and tendons.

Incline dumbbell curls bring Tom's massive biceps into powerful contraction. (*Mike Neveux*)

There are many books for stretching exercises. The best is Bob Anderson's *Stretching* (Fullerton, CA: Anderson, 1975), which is available in major book shops. Pick out one or two stretching exercises for each part of your body in order to formulate a personal flexibility program.

The best prestretching warm-up is simple walking. After you've spent five to ten minutes walking, slowly begin each stretching movement, hold it for a few counts just short of the point where you feel pain, back off for a few moments, then repeat the stretched position. Never bounce a stretch, since any bouncing movements can create injuries in your muscles and joints.

It takes time to feel results from your stretching program. Certainly, you won't have dramatic or quick gains in flexibility like your gains in strength and muscle mass from your bodybuilding workouts. By preventing injuries and allowing for stronger contractions over an extended range of motion, flexibility training definitely makes you a better bodybuilder.

Stretch Marks

Virtually all bodybuilders have stretch marks, which are initially reddish or purplish tears in your skin that eventually turn almost white (the color of all scars). Stretch marks occur when your muscles (and often fatty tissues) expand too rapidly for your skin to accommodate the expansion. (Pregnant women inevitably get stretch marks on their lower abdomens.)

I've seen some bodybuilders with very few stretch marks, while others have the marks even on their forearms and calves. Stretch marks can be minimized, if not actually prevented, by following a few simple precautions.

First, it's a mistake to gain weight too quickly. A massive weight gain is largely body fat rather than muscle, which inevitably results in stretch marks. I also feel that you must supplement your diet with vitamins and minerals. If your skin isn't healthy, it's more likely to tear.

Finally, it's important to keep your skin moisturized. I put Nivea moisturizing cream on my skin every time I take a shower, and I feel it's helped me to keep my stretch marks under control. And if you do start to develop a stretch mark, you can minimize it by rubbing Vitamin E cream over the injured area several times per day. The vitamin E cream will both help to keep your skin moist and supple, and help to heal the skin tears.

Supination

One secret of effective biceps training is hand supination during curling exercises. Everyone knows that the biceps contract to bend your arms. However, most bodybuilders don't understand that the biceps also contract to help supinate your hand. Supination is a rotation of your wrist until your palm is facing forward when your arm is down.

You can't supinate your hands when you do barbell curls, so it's obvious that you'll get a lot more out of performing dumbbell curls for your biceps. An E-Z curl bar is the worst thing to use for biceps development because it actually locks your hands away from a supinated position.

When I do dumbbell curls, I start the movement with my palms facing towards my legs. Then about halfway up in the movement, I rotate my hands 90 degrees to the supinated position. This supination movement has done wonders in building up my biceps over the past few years.

Injuries

Every bodybuilder periodically suffers from training injuries. I've had my share over the years, ranging from minor aches and pains to a completely ruptured right biceps tendon just prior to the 1982 Mr. Olympia competition.

I take even the most serious injuries philosophically. Things always work out for the best, so I keep an open mind. I look at the positive side, even though it's difficult to do when there are so many negative aspects to a situation. Something always goes wrong sooner or later. Everyone has problems, and you have to overcome them. That's an imperative in bodybuilding.

Minor, nagging injuries can generally be ignored. As long as the pain does not become more severe as you train a muscle group, a sore joint is merely a minor annoyance. But be sure that you thoroughly warm up an injured area, and terminate a workout that stresses any injury which becomes progressively more painful.

Major injuries should *never* be self-treated. Any long-term or major injury should be treated by a physician specializing in sports medicine. And his advice should be strictly followed. Nothing is more foolish than to risk your health because of an injury that could have been easily treated. See a doctor!

4 Off-Season Exercises & Routines

Let's get down to the actual business of training during an off-season cycle. You will find detailed descriptions and illustrations of the 20 exercises that I consider to be best for off-season use in this chapter. If you're new to bodybuilding, it's essential that you learn to correctly perform these movements because dangerous and unproductive training habits will be difficult to break later on. If you are an experienced bodybuilder, I'm sure that you'll enjoy reading about the fine points of performing each of these exercises that have allowed me to build one of the world's most massive, proportionate, and muscular physiques.

At the end of the chapter, I will give you three routines that include these exercises—one for beginners, one for more advanced bodybuilders, and one that I use during my off-season cycle. If you follow each of these training programs for several months, I can virtually guarantee that you'll make great gains from your training. Perhaps you will soon win the bodybuilding title that has eluded you in previous attempts.

There are two primary goals to have during an off-season cycle. First, you must seek to steadily increase your overall muscle mass. And second, you must use the muscle-priority training procedure outlined in Chapter 1 to improve any weak body parts. The training programs presented in this chapter are intended to give you balanced development; you may need to adjust them to apply either additional training volume, or greater workout intensity without adding exercises to your program.

Start/Finish

Squats

Values. I believe that squats are the single best lower-body movement, and probably the best exercise for your entire body. Primary stress is placed on the quadriceps muscles on the front of your thighs, buttocks, and erector spinae muscles. Secondary stress is on your hamstrings, upper-back muscles, and abdominals.

Starting Point. Place a barbell on a squat rack and load it up with your desired poundage. Place your feet directly under the bar, bend your legs and dip your head beneath the bar, and position the bar across your trapezius muscles behind your neck. To balance the weight across your shoulders, grasp the bar halfway between them and the barbell plates on each side. Straighten your legs to lift the bar off the rack and step back two or three feet from the rack. Set your feet about shoulder-width apart, your toes angled slightly outward. Tense your back muscles and keep your torso as upright as possible during the exercise. You can help keep your torso upright by focussing your eyes on a spot on the wall at head level as you perform squats.

Movement Performance. Slowly bend your legs and lower your body down into as deep a squatting position as you can. Without bouncing at the bottom of the movement, slowly straighten your legs and return to the starting point. Repeat the movement for the suggested number of repetitions.

Training Tips. Before you begin your heavy squats, it's essential that you spend at least ten minutes stretching your quads, hamstrings, and hip muscles. Do freehand squats and light, high-rep squats to fully warm up your joints and muscles. If you find it difficult to balance your body as you do squats, you can wear shoes with slightly elevated heels. However, I believe that it's better to squat flat-footed with shoes having no built-up heels. With heavier poundages, you should wear a weightlifting belt cinched tightly around your waist to help support your lower back and abdomen during the exercise.

Comments. Many bodybuilders do partial squats, going only half or three-quarters of the way down, or squatting only until their thighs are parallel to the floor. However, the key in using the squat exercise is to always bend your legs as fully as possible and go as deeply as you can into the movement. Some bodybuilders avoid squats because they feel the movement will overdevelop their butt and make their hips wider—neither of which the exercise will do—or they're worried the movement will damage their knees. As long as you avoid bouncing in the low position of the exercise, however, squats can't damage your knees. The truth is that you will probably *never* reach your full bodybuilding potential without performing the squat.

Midpoint

Start

Leg Extensions

Values. This is a very direct isolation exercise for the quadriceps muscles at the front of your thighs. Leg extensions allow you to carve deep grooves of muscularity between the major muscle groups of your quads.

Starting Point. There is a large variety of leg-extension machines, but you'll probably find the Nautilus machine works your quads most effectively. Sit in the machine and adjust the back of the seat until your butt is up against it when your knees are firmly against the padded edge towards the lever arm at the right side of the apparatus. Slide your toes and insteps beneath the roller pads attached to the end of the machine's lever arm and fasten the seat belt firmly over your lap. Grasp the handles at the side of the seat to steady your body in position during the exercise.

Movement Performance. Now slowly straighten your legs completely, holding the top (peak contracted) position of the movement for a slow count of two to maximize the effect of the exercise. Slowly lower back to the starting position and repeat the movement for the required number of repetitions. You'll see a lot of bodybuilders do this movement with a very quick and jerky cadence, but I believe in slow and controlled raising *and* lowering of the resistance in order to place maximum stress on the working muscles.

Training Tips. You can isolate stress on different areas of your quads according to how you hold your feet as you do leg extensions. Most bodybuilders will point their toes straight upwards during the exercise, but you can angle your feet so your toes point either inward or outward at about 45-degree angles. Pointing your toes outward places greater stress on your vastus medialis muscle, the part of your quadriceps group that lies just above your knee on the inner edge of your thigh. In contrast, pointing your toes inward places greater stress on the lower and outer section of your quads just above your knee joint.

Finish

Leg Curls

Values. This is a very direct isolation exercise for the biceps femoris (also called the thigh biceps or hamstrings) muscle group at the back of your thighs.

Starting Point. There is a large variety of leg-curl machines, but I recommend the Nautilus machine. Lie face down on the flat, padded surface of the machine with your knees at the edge of the pad towards the lever arm of the apparatus. Hook your heels under the roller pads of the machine and fully extend your legs. Grasp the handles at the sides of the machine to steady your body in position as you do the exercise.

Start

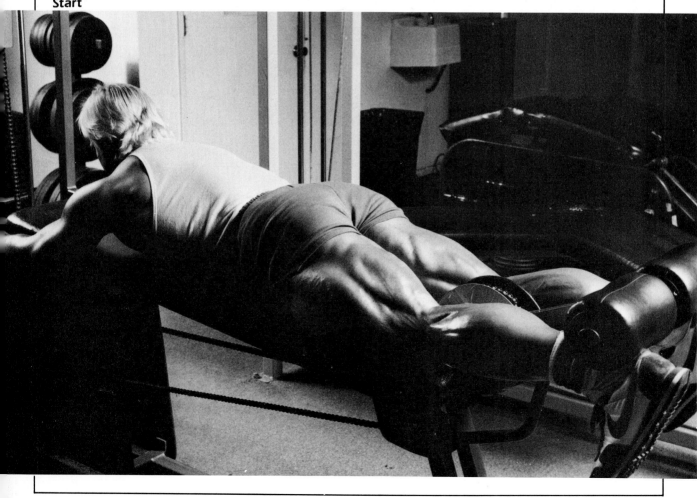

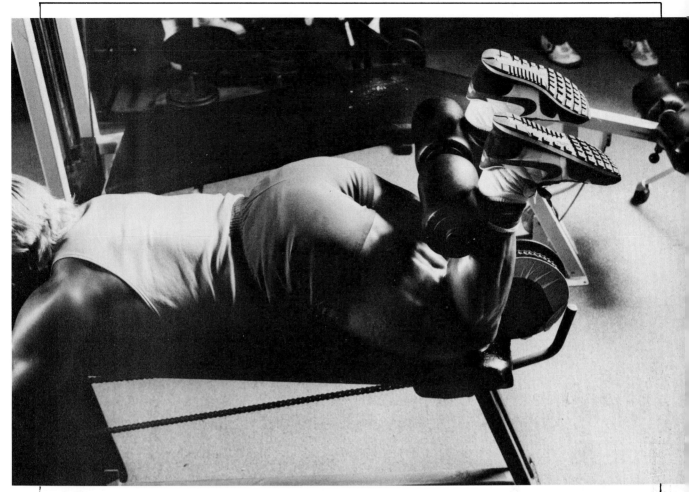

Finish

Movement Performance. Make sure that your hips are held firmly against the surface of the machine, and slowly bend your legs as completely as possible. Hold the top position of the movement for a slow count of two to maximize the peak contraction effect of the exercise. Slowly lower the weight back to the starting point, and repeat the movement for an appropriate number of repetitions.

Training Tips. You can vary the angle of your feet during the movement to attack specific areas of your thigh biceps. Also, it's important that you keep your feet flexed (the opposite of pointing your toes) during the exercise to isolate your calves from the movement.

Start

Standing Calf Raises

Values. If you want to develop diamond-shaped calves, this is the movement that will do it for you. Calf raises performed on a standing calf machine directly stress the gastrocnemius muscles of your calves in relative isolation from the rest of your body.

Starting Point. Bend your legs and place your shoulders in a comfortable position under the yokes of the machine. Grasp the horizontal bars attached to the yokes to steady your body in position as you do the exercise. Place your toes and the balls of your feet on the calf block of the machine, your feet set about shoulder-width apart. Straighten your body to bear the weight of the machine and allow your heels to sink as far below the level of your toes as possible to fully stretch your calf muscles.

Movement Performance. Rise up as high as you can on your toes in one slow, smooth movement. Slowly lower to the position in which your calves are completely stretched and repeat the exercise. It's essential that you do this movement with as exaggerated a range of motion as possible, without pausing along the full range of motion.

Training Tips. Many bodybuilders will tell you to alternate sets performed with your toes pointed straight ahead, angled inward at 45-degree angles and pointed outward at 45-degree angles. However, I have never discovered any benefit from changing toe angles; I perform all of my

Finish

sets with my toes pointed directly ahead or slightly outward. One productive way of stressing your calves from new angles is to vary the width of your foot placement on the calf block. You'll feel the movement much differently when you have your feet close together than when you do the exercise with your feet set 4–6 inches (10–15 cm) wider than the width of your shoulders on each side.

Deadlifts

Values. This is an excellent basic exercise that powerfully stresses all of the muscles of your lower back, hip girdle, and forearms. Significant secondary stress is placed on your upper-back and thigh muscles.

Starting Point. Stand on the floor with your shins touching a heavy barbell. Bend your knees and bend over at the waist to take a mixed grip on the bar (one hand forward and the other hand facing the rear), your hands set slightly wider

Start

Midpoint

than your shoulders. It's important that your hand with the strongest grip be the one with your palm facing forward. Keep your arms straight throughout the movement. Arch your back and bend your knees until your torso is at an approximate 45-degree angle with the floor when your arms are held straight. This is the basic pulling position to use whenever you lift any heavy weight from the floor, so observe it carefully in the exercise photos.

Movement Performance. Slowly lift the weight from the floor by first straightening your legs, then follow through by straightening your torso until you are standing erect with the weight resting across your upper thighs. Lower the barbell back to the floor by reversing the movement. Repeat the exercise for the required number of reps.

Training Tips. When I'm doing heavy deadlifts, I imagine that all I must do is try to push my feet through the floor, and this makes it easier to lift the weight. If you know how to use lifting straps to secure your grip to the bar, you can do deadlifts with both palms facing your legs or the mixed grip described above. You can also do stiff-legged deadlifts with a much lighter weight while standing on a flat exercise bench or thick block of wood. Stiff-legged deadlifts place much more stress on your hamstrings in comparison to the regular deadlift performed with bent legs.

Front Chins

Values. This is principally a lat movement that develops width in your upper back. Secondary emphasis is on your biceps, brachialis, and posterior deltoid muscle groups. Generally speaking, chins and pulldowns are movements that develop the upper back, while bent rows and similar exercises primarily develop thickness in the upper-back muscles.

Starting Point. Reach up and take an overgrip on the bar in which your hands are set 3–4 inches (7–10 cm) wider on each side than your shoulders. Straighten your arms completely and stretch your lats at the beginning of the exercise. You can probably do the movement most comfortably if you bend your legs at right angles and cross your ankles.

Movement Performance. Concentrate on pulling your elbows both downwards and backwards; bend your arms and slowly pull yourself up to the bar, trying to touch your chest to the bar. Be sure that your back is arched in the top position of this movement. Lower back to the starting point and repeat the exercise.

Training Tips. If you don't have sufficient strength to perform at least five or six front chins in the manner just described, you should work hard at doing front lat pulldowns with heavy weights to develop this strength. You can also perform chins behind the neck in which you pull your body up to touch your trapezius to the bar rather than your chest. Regardless of the type of chin you perform, you can vary the width of your grip while doing the movement to stress your lats from different angles.

Start

Finish

Start

Barbell Bent Rows

Values. This excellent movement places primary stress on your latissimus dorsi, trapezius, biceps, and brachialis muscles. Significant secondary stress is placed on your erector spinae, posterior deltoid, and forearm muscles. Overall, barbell bent rows, bench presses, and parallel bar dips are the best all-around upper-body movements.

Starting Point. Stand on the floor about a foot and a half back from a moderately heavy barbell. Bend over and take a shoulder-width overgrip on the barbell and set your feet about shoulder-width apart. Keep your legs slightly bent throughout your set to remove potentially harmful stress from your lower back. Straighten your arms and raise your torso upwards until it is parallel to the floor and maintain this torso position throughout the movement. Your back should also be held in a slightly arched position during the exercise. If you are using large-diameter plates on the bar, they might not be clear of the floor in this starting position. If this is the case, you should perform your barbell bent rows while standing on a flat exercise bench or thick block of wood.

Movement Performance. Keeping your elbows in close to your body, slowly bend your arms and pull the barbell upwards to touch the lower part of your rib cage. Be sure to emphasize your back arch in the top position of the exercise, squeezing all of your back muscles as tightly as you can when they are fully contracted. Slowly lower the bar back down to the floor and repeat the exercise.

Training Tips. It's important to think about *squeezing* your muscles in all exercises, particularly in back movements. And at the other end of the movement, it's essential that you completely stretch

Finish

your lats at the beginning of each repetition. And, as with all body parts, it's important to be able to contract and mentally feel each movement without resistance before actually performing the exercise with a weight.

You can use either a narrow grip with your hands actually touching in the middle of the bar for bent rows, as wide a grip as the length of the barbell will permit, or any grip in between these two extremes. Each change of grip width attacks your upper-back muscles from a distinctly different angle. You can perform similar rowing movements with a pair of dumbbells, a floor pulley, a high pulley, a single dumbbell, or a T-bar apparatus.

Finally, you should wear a weightlifting belt when you do your heaviest sets of barbell bent rows. The belt will help support and protect your back.

Bench Presses

Values. This excellent basic movement for your upper body places intense stress on your pectorals, anterior deltoids, and triceps. Significant secondary emphasis is on the medial deltoid, serratus, latissimus dorsi, and other back muscles that rotate your scapulae. Since this is such a fundamental upper-body movement, be sure to do plenty of warmups prior to tackling the heavy weights.

Starting Point. Place a barbell on a bench support rack and load it up with an appropriate poundage. Lie back on the bench with your shoulders 3–4 inches (7–10 cm) from the rack supports and place your feet flat on the floor on either side of the bench to balance your body in position during the exercise. Take an overgrip on the barbell with your hands set only 2–3 inches (5–7 cm) wider than your shoulders on each side. Straighten your arms to press the weight

Start/Finish

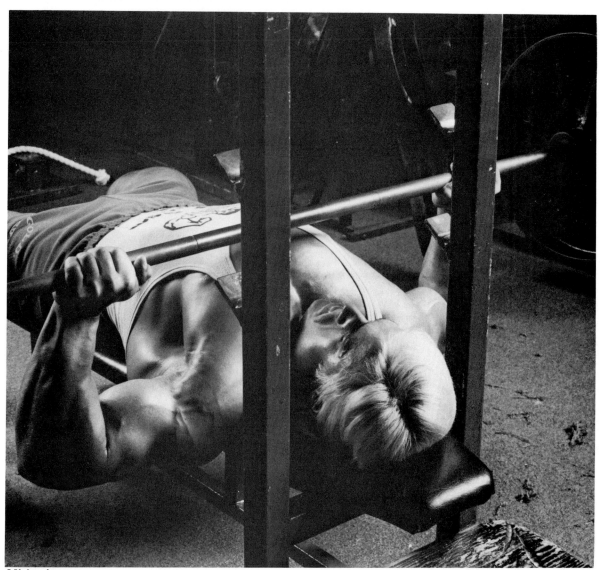

Midpoint

from the rack with locked elbows directly above your shoulder joints.

Movement Performance. Making sure that your upper arms travel directly out to the sides at right angles to your torso, slowly bend your arms and lower the barbell downwards to lightly touch the middle of your chest. Without bouncing the bar off your chest, deliberately press the barbell until your elbows lock. Repeat the exercise for the desired number of repetitions.

Training Tips. You'll often see bodybuilders lifting their hips from the bench and severely arching their backs to enable them to use heavier weights on their bench presses, but it's much better to use strict exercise form and have a partner give you forced reps. In any case, it's essential that you have an alert spotter standing at the head end of the bench when you use heavy poundages. Should you fail with a heavy rep, he can rescue you by lifting the bar from your chest.

Start/Finish

Parallel Bar Dips

Values. This is another excellent basic exercise that intensely stresses your pectorals (particularly the lower and outer sections of the muscle group), anterior delts, and triceps. Secondary stress is on your medial deltoids and the muscles of your back that rotate your scapulae.

Starting Point. There are two types of parallel bar assemblies, one in which the bars actually are parallel and another with the bars angled inward towards one end, which permits a variety of grip widths. If you use the angled set of bars, be sure to position your body so your hands are set only a bit wider than your shoulders on each side. Jump up and support yourself on straight arms, your palms facing inward as you grasp the bars. Bend your knees at 90-degree angles and cross your feet during the movement. Be sure that your torso is inclined forward at the head end as you perform the dips. You *can* do dips with your torso upright, but this movement is primarily for your triceps.

Movement Performance. Keeping your elbows in at the sides of your torso, slowly bend your arms and lower your body as far down between the bars as is comfortably possible. Slowly push yourself back up to the starting point and repeat the movement for the required number of reps.

Training Tips. You'll soon be able to do more than 10–12 reps in a set of parallel bar dips. At that point, you should begin to add resistance to the movement by attaching a light dumbbell to a loop of rope or nylon webbing encircling your waist. The dumbbell should hang down in front of your legs, and you can steady it in position by crossing your thighs over the weight. If you want to perform

Midpoint

forced reps, your training partner should stand behind you and merely grasp your feet in his hands. Then you can use thigh strength to assist your pecs, delts, and triceps in completing a couple of forced reps.

Flat-Bench Dumbbell Flyes

Values. This movement isolates stress more on your pectorals and anterior del-toids and less on your triceps. Even though this is an isolation movement for your chest, you'll be able to use substantial weights with some practice.

Start

Finish

Starting Point. Grasp two moderately heavy dumbbells in your hands, lie back on a flat bench with your feet placed firmly on the floor to balance your body, and extend your arms straight upwards from your shoulders with your palms facing towards each other. Bend your arms slightly throughout your set. I also prefer to do my flyes with my wrists flexed at the bottom point of the movement.

Movement Performance. Keeping your elbows back at all times, slowly lower the dumbbells out to the sides and downwards to as low a position as is comfort-ably possible. In this position, you should feel a strong stretch in your pectorals. Use pec strength to move the dumbbells back along the same arcs and upwards until they almost touch each other directly above the middle of your chest. Repeat the exercise.

Training Tips. By placing a four-inch square block of wood under either the head or foot end of your flat exercise bench, you can do flyes on a slight incline or decline. Incline flyes shift stress more to the upper pecs; decline flyes primarily emphasize the lower and outer sections of your pectorals.

Cross-Bench Pullovers

Values. This movement stresses the entire upper torso, particularly the pectorals, serratus muscles, and latissimus dorsi group. I don't particularly subscribe to the idea that you can enlarge the volume of your rib cage by doing pullovers. If you work your chest and back in the same bodybuilding training session, cross-bench pullovers would be a good transition movement between the two body parts.

Starting Point. Place a moderately heavy dumbbell on end about a third of

Start/Finish

Midpoint

the way from one end of a flat exercise bench. Lie with your upper torso across the middle of the bench and place your feet flat on the floor in a manner that moves your shins to a vertical position. Reach over and place your palms flat against the undersides of the upper set of plates on the dumbbell and encircle the dumbbell bar with your thumbs to keep it from slipping out of your hands during the movement. Move the dumbbell from the bench to a position directly above your shoulder joints.

Movement Performance. Simultaneously bend your arms about 15 degrees and lower the dumbbell rearwards and downwards to as low a position as possible. Keep your elbows in towards the midline of your body as you lower and then raise the weight. Move the dumbbell back along the same arc to the starting point, simultaneously straightening your arms.

Training Tips. To get a better stretch in your working muscles at the bottom point of the movement, you can drop your hips 3–4 inches (7–10 cm) as you reach the low point of the exercise. You can also do dumbbell or barbell pullovers lying lengthwise on an exercise bench, but you won't get as much out of the movement.

Military Presses

Values. This is the most basic of all shoulder exercises. It intensely stresses your anterior and medial deltoids in conjunction with your triceps. Significant secondary stress is placed on the upper-chest and upper-back muscles.

Starting Point. Stand on the floor with your shins against a barbell and take an overgrip on the bar with your hands set 3–4 inches (7–10 cm) wider than your shoulders on each side. Straighten your arms, dip your hips, and pull the barbell quickly up to your shoulders with a coordinated action of your legs, back, and arms. Rotate your elbows directly beneath the bar. Stand erect with your feet set about shoulder-width apart.

Movement Performance. Without allowing your torso to bend rearwards, slowly straighten your arms and push the barbell straight up past your face until your elbows lock directly above your

Start

Finish

shoulders. Slowly lower the weight back to the starting point and repeat the movement for the suggested number of repetitions.

Training Tips. Rather than cleaning the bar from the floor to your shoulders at the beginning of each repetition, you can merely take the bar off of a squat rack at the beginning of each set and then replace it on the rack when you have done your reps. You can also isolate your legs from the movement by pressing while seated on a flat exercise bench, but I recommend the standing version of the movement.

Start

Dumbbell Side Laterals

Values. This is an isolation exercise that strongly attacks the medial heads of your deltoids. I simply don't feel that you can get the full, rounded look in your delts during an off-season cycle when performing just pressing movements. This is why I list side laterals as an off-season exercise.

Starting Point. Grasp two moderately heavy dumbbells, set your feet about shoulder-width apart, and stand erect. Bend slightly forward at the waist and maintain this torso lean throughout your set. With your palms facing each other, press the dumbbells together 3–4 inches (7–10 cm) in front of your hips. Bend your arms slightly and keep them rounded throughout the movement.

Movement Performance. Now, without swinging the weights, raise them slowly out to the sides and slightly forward in semicircular arcs from the starting position until they are slightly above shoulder height. As you do the movement, your palms should be facing towards the floor and in the top position of the exercise, your thumb must be slightly lower than your little finger to isolate stress on your medial deltoids. Slowly lower the dumbbells back along the same arcs to the starting point and repeat the movement for an appropriate number of repetitions.

Training Tips. The most common mistakes in this exercise are swinging the weights upwards using a body cheat and lifting them primarily with your anterior delts by having your thumb above the level of your little finger on each hand. For greater concentration on the movement, you can do it one arm at a time while steadying yourself against a sturdy upright post with your free hand.

On one-armed and one-legged movements you don't need to split your focus between two limbs, which allows you to concentrate more deeply on the working muscles, resulting in greater muscle-building stimulation. You can do one-arm side laterals either with your torso bolt upright, or leaning slightly away from the upright post you're holding, which changes the deltoid stress a bit.

Finish

Barbell Curls

Values. This is the most basic of all biceps exercises. It directly stresses the biceps and places secondary emphasis on the powerful flexor muscles on the inner sides of your forearms.

Starting Point. Take a shoulder-width undergrip on a barbell, set your feet a comfortable distance apart, and stand

Start

Near Finish

erect. Your arms should be straight down at your sides with the barbell resting across your upper thighs. Pin your upper arms against the sides of your torso as you do the exercise.

Movement Performance. Without allowing your torso to move, slowly bend your arms and curl the barbell in a semicircular arc from your thighs up to a point just beneath your chin. Slowly lower the bar back to the starting point and repeat the movement.

Training Tips. If you have difficulty restraining your torso movement, you should do barbell curls with your back resting against either a wall or a sturdy upright post in the gym. This effectively keeps torso movement from helping you to curl the barbell upwards. You can achieve different stresses in your biceps by moving your grip either inward or outward. Arnold Schwarzenegger consistently favors a wide grip for his barbell curls, and his biceps are beyond comparison.

Start

Dumbbell Curls

Values. Dumbbell curls stress the same muscles as barbell curls; however, you can supinate your hands as you do dumbbell curls. Most bodybuilders fail to realize that the biceps have two functions—arm flexion and hand supination. Supination involves turning your palm from a position facing the floor when your arm is bent at a right angle to a position in which your palm is facing directly upwards. Obviously, you can't do this movement when your grip is fixed in position by a straight exercise bar.

Starting Point. Grasp two moderately heavy dumbbells and sit at the end of a flat exercise bench (I prefer to do this movement seated on a bench with an upright back that supports my torso in a vertical position during the movement). Hang your arms straight down at your sides, your palms facing towards each other. Pin your upper arms against the sides of your torso throughout the exercise.

Movement Performance. Slowly curl the dumbbells forward and upwards in semicircular arcs, simultaneously supinating your hands so your palms are facing upwards during at least the last half of the exercise. Slowly lower the dumbbells back to the starting point and repeat the exercise. Tense your biceps as you contract them.

Training Tips. You can also do seated dumbbell curls in alternate fashion, one dumbbell being curled upwards as the other is lowered. And you can perform standing dumbbell curls either alternately or together.

Finish

Barbell Triceps Extensions

Values. This is a good isolation movement that builds a high degree of mass in your triceps muscles.

Starting Point. Take a narrow overgrip in the middle of a barbell (there should be about 6 inches [15 cm] of space showing between your index fingers). Stand erect with your arms straight and the bar directly above your head.

Movement Performance. Without moving your upper arms, slowly bend your forearms and lower the barbell rearwards and downwards in a semicircular arc until your hands touch the back of your neck. Use your triceps to move the bar back along the same arc to the starting position and repeat the movement for an appropriate number of repetitions.

Training Tips. This movement can also be performed in a seated position, or while lying on a flat, incline, or decline bench. Each variation of barbell triceps extensions hits your triceps muscles a bit differently.

Start

Finish

Start

Pulley Pushdowns

Values. This is an excellent isolation movement for your triceps that places particular emphasis on the outer head of the muscle group.

Starting Point. I use a short, straight bar handle attached to an overhead pulley to perform this movement. Take a medium overgrip on the handle and place your feet shoulder-width apart about a foot back from the handle. Bend your arms fully and pin your upper arms to the sides of your torso with your upper arms perpendicular to the floor. Lean slightly forward at the waist. At the beginning of this movement, your hands should be holding the bar just under your chin.

Movement Performance. Without moving your upper arms, slowly straighten your arms and move the handle in a semicircular arc down to your thighs. Slowly return your hands back to the starting point and repeat the exercise.

Training Tips. You can use a rope handle that places your hands in a parallel grip, or a short bar handle that is angled downwards at each end. I can't seem to isolate my triceps unless I use a straight bar handle, but you should explore all of the available variations of each exercise. One of these other two handles may be much better for your unique structure than the straight handle. And doing half or quarter reps (called "burns") at the end of a set can be very effective.

Finish

Barbell Wrist Curls

Start

Values. Performed with your palms facing upwards, barbell wrist curls stress the powerful flexor muscles on the inner sides of your forearms. And when done with your palms facing towards the floor, barbell wrist curls place direct stress on the somewhat weaker extensor muscles on the outer sides of your forearms.

Starting Point. Take a narrow undergrip in the middle of a bar (there should be about 6 inches [15 cm] of space showing between your little fingers). Sit straddling the bench and run your forearms down the bench so your fists are hanging off the end of it.

Finish 2

Finish 1

Movement Performance. Flex your wrists upwards as far as possible, curling the barbell in a small semicircular arc to as high a position as possible. Lower back to the starting point and repeat the movement for the suggested number of reps.

Training Tips. When you perform this movement with your palms towards the floor, you might find it more effective if you kneel beside the bench and run your forearms across it rather than along it. You can also do the palms-up movement with a dumbbell, one arm at a time, with your forearm along the bench.

Roman Chair Sit-Ups

Values. Roman chair sit-ups stress the entire frontal abdominal wall (rectus abdominis), especially the upper part of your abs.

Starting Point. Sit on a Roman chair bench and wedge your toes beneath the foot restraint bar in front. Cross your arms on your chest throughout each set.

Movement Performance. Incline your torso rearwards until it is slightly below an imaginary line drawn at a 45-degree angle with the floor. Sit back just until you begin to feel tension coming off your abdominals (this will be somewhat short

Start/Finish

of the position when you are sitting erect). Rock slowly back and forth between this point and the low position until you have finished doing the suggested number of repetitions.

Training Tips. At the beginning level of training, you should do this movement without twisting. But once you are more advanced, you can twist to each side on successive reps to involve your intercostal muscles more intensely in the movement. To increase the intensity of this movement, you can place a four-inch square block of wood beneath the foot end of the Roman chair. Alternatively, you can hold a light barbell plate on your chest.

Midpoint

Bench Leg Raises

Values. All leg raises stress the entire rectus abdominis wall, especially the lower sections of your frontal abdominals.

Starting Point. Lie on your back on a flat exercise bench with your hips right at one end of the bench. Reach behind your head and grasp the edges of the bench to steady your body in position during the exercise. Bend your legs slightly and hold your heels just clear of the floor. You can either press your legs together during this exercise or cross your ankles.

Start

Movement Performance. Using your frontal abdominals, raise your feet in a semicircular arc from the starting point to a position directly above your hips. Lower slowly back to the starting point, making sure that your heels don't rest on the floor, and repeat the movement for the desired number of repetitions.

Training Tips. It's also possible to do this exercise while lying on an inclined abdominal board, but incline leg raises don't give you the long range of movement inherent in bench leg raises. To add intensity to bench leg raises, you can hold a light dumbbell between your feet as you perform the movement.

Finish

Level-One Off-Season Workout

You'll need at least six weeks of steady training on a normal beginning-level bodybuilding routine before you attack the heavier workout presented in this section. You will need at least six more weeks of steady workouts to condition your body to handle the heavy work load of the Level-Two routine.

MONDAY
(Legs, Chest, Abs)

	Sets	Reps
Squats (warm up, then work up to . . .)	3	5
Additional Squats	1	10*
Leg Curls	2	10†
Bench Presses (warm up, then work up to . . .)	5	5
Roman Chair Sit-ups	3	20–30
Standing Calf Raises	3	12–15

WEDNESDAY
(Back, Shoulders, Arms, Abs, Calves)

	Sets	Reps
Deadlifts (warm up, then work up to . . .)	2	5
Front Chins	3	max
Barbell Bent Rows	3	6–8
Military Presses	3	6–8
Cross-bench Pullovers (moderate weight)	2	max
Standing Alternate Dumbbell Curls	3	6–8†
Pulley Pushdowns	3	8–12†
Bench Leg Raises	3	25–30
Seated Calf Raises	3	10–12†

FRIDAY (All Body Parts)

	Sets	Reps
Bench Presses (warm up, then work up to . . .)	3	3
Additional Bench Presses	1	15*
Front Chins	3	max
Seated Press Behind Neck	3	6–8
Cross-bench Pullovers	3	max
Standing Barbell Curls	3	6–8†
Lying Barbell Triceps Extensions	3	8–12†
Squats (warm up, then work up to . . .)	2	15†
Leg Curls	2	15†
Roman Chair Sit-ups	3	25–30
Standing Calf Raises	3	12–15

*With a moderate weight only, as a warm-down set.
†Continue each set to failure.

I've presented a couple of exercises in this routine that I didn't explain in this chapter. You will find explanations and illustrations of presses behind neck and seated calf raises in Chapter 7. If you don't wish to use these two movements at this level, you can do military presses and standing calf raises instead.

Level-Two Off-Season Workout

After three months of progressively heavier training on the foregoing routine, you will be ready to attack the split-routine program outlined in this section. Alternatively, this is the type of off-season routine that I would recommend for use by anyone who has from one to four years of steady training behind him.

The program in this section may seem quite simple to many readers. It's no-frills training, to say the least, but I don't believe in some of the intricate mass- and power-building routines that many top bodybuilders recommend. The key to making gains is not how intricate your routine is, but how hard you train.

As a final note, you should always start major sets (i.e., those done for three sets of three reps, three sets of five reps, etc.) with a *light* weight. This enables you to increase your top weight on these major exercises by five or ten pounds each week with little difficulty. This system of working up from a low poundage to a new personal best in each exercise over an eight- to ten-week period of time is a method widely used in powerlifting. And as a former powerlifter, I have successfully adapted the method for use in bodybuilding.

MONDAY
(Chest, Back, Shoulders, Abs)

	Sets	Reps
Bench Presses (warm up, then work up to . . .)	3	3
Additional Bench Presses	1	10*
Dumbbell Flyes (low incline)	2	8–12†
Chins Behind Neck	3	max
Barbell Bent Rows	3	10–12
Cross-bench Pullovers	2	15
Seated Press Behind Neck	3	6–8†
Dumbbell Bent Laterals	2	15
Roman Chair Sit-ups	3–4	25–30

TUESDAY
(Legs and Arms)

	Sets	Reps
Squats (warm up, then work up to . . .)	3	3
Hack Squats	2	6–8†
Leg Curls	2	10–15†
Standing Calf Raises	3–6	6–20
Seated Dumbbell Curls	3–5	6–8†
Pulley Pushdowns	3–5	10–12†

THURSDAY
(Back, Chest, Shoulders, Abs)

	Sets	Reps
Deadlifts (warm up, then work up to . . .)	1	3
Front Chins	3	max
Barbell Bent Rows	3	6–8†
Cross-bench Pullovers	2	15
Bench Presses (warm up, then work up to . . .)	3	5
Incline Flyes	2	10–15†
Seated Press Behind Neck	3	10–12
Dumbbell Bent Laterals	2	15
Bench Leg Raises	3–5	25–30

FRIDAY
(Arms and Legs)

	Sets	Reps
Seated Dumbbell Curls	5	6–8†
Pulley Pushdowns	5	10–12†
Squats (warm up first)	2	15†
Hack Squats	3	6–8†
Leg Curls	2	15†
Seated Calf Raises	3–6	6–20

*With a moderate weight only, as a warm-down set.
†Continue to failure.

With minor adjustments, you can use this routine for up to two years with good results. Just keep pushing to add weight to the bar, and always try to do your first few reps—as well as all of your heaviest sets—in strict form.

Tom Platz's Off-Season Routine

I'm sure that you're eager to learn about my off-season workouts. If you'll accept a couple of preconditions, I'll be happy to outline a sample routine. First, you must keep in mind that I have been training steadily and progressively more intensely for nearly eighteen years. As a result, my recuperative powers are much greater than yours and I can make good gains from a workout schedule that would almost kill a lot of less experienced bodybuilders.

Second, I change my training programs frequently, so what you see listed here may not be what I am doing at Gold's Gym or the World Gym the next time you happen to see me work out. To keep mentally interested in my workouts, I find that I must constantly vary them a little from one day to the next.

You will see from the following workout that I train on a five-day cycle in the off-season. This involves four consecutive training days for various parts of my body, followed by one day of rest. Of course, this means that I have to train on a lot of weekends, but I'm a professional and my bodybuilding progress is what matters most to me, so I'm willing to give up my weekends to train.

While I train consistently heavy and with consistently high intensity, I do tend to cycle my training intensity. Very simply, I am unable to maintain absolute peak training intensity for more than six to eight weeks before burning out both mentally and physically, so I intersperse periods of lower workout intensity lasting four to six weeks between my cycles of absolute intensity training.

You should also understand my concept of a perfect, high-intensity set, as I perform it in my own training routines. To me, a perfect set involves taking an exercise to positive-rep failure, while at the same time feeling the negative half of the movement as deeply as possible in the working muscles. After I reach positive failure, I reach for negative failure by either cheating or getting assistance through the positive half of the

exercise, then lowering the weight by myself while mightily resisting its downward momentum with all of the power that I can summon.

My perfect set concludes with me holding the weight in the fully contracted or fully extended position of the exercise, thinking about stretching the muscle with the resistance I hold in my hands. I hold the weight until I literally can't hold it at all, until it can't be moved in any way; if someone helped me up with the weight, I literally couldn't slow it down as it descended. *That* is intensity!

On some exercises—such as incline dumbbell presses—I do partial reps every second workout prior to just holding the weight as described in the previous paragraph. A common mistake made by young bodybuilders who have seen me train is to do partial reps without first fully exhausting a muscle group with full positive and negative reps. They see me a couple of minutes into a set when I'm forcing out all of the partials I can get, and they forget that I have already gone to both positive and negative failure. The partials themselves won't do that much for you, but tacked on to the end of a set that has already been taken to failure, they greatly increase training intensity.

Remember that a novice bodybuilder trains by the numbers, just as a beginning artist paints by the numbers. But as an artist grows more experienced and matures, he eventually forgets all about the numbers and his or her paintings grow uniquely from the artist's inner feelings, until ultimately the student has become a master with his own unique style of painting.

Beginning bodybuilders are very similar to novice painters. They eventually become oblivious to numbers (sets, reps, and even training poundages), creating physiques that are expressions of their own inner visualizations. Being an artist as well as an athlete, a bodybuilder must constantly relate to his or her inner feelings. A truly intelligent bodybuilder carefully monitors every muscle contraction and physiological response to exercise, how a weight feels on a particular day, how fast the weight is moving in an exercise, and a host of other biofeedback data.

There is absolutely no question in my mind that bodybuilding is truly a sport, an art form, *and* a science. After many years of consistent and dedicated training, you will combine these three disciplines to become very proficient at "feeling" (or sensing) the effect of your training, diet, recuperative process, and psychological approach to your sport. You'll develop an amazingly accurate instinct for evaluating every aspect of your sports preparation.

Let's take an example of training instinct in action. While I normally follow a five-day training cycle—four days of training followed by one rest day—my instincts occasionally tell me to take two or three rest days rather than one before resuming the training cycle. At other times, my training instinct suggests that I should skip the rest day and immediately resume my four consecutive days of training.

When I've ignored my instincts, I've either burned out and briefly lost my enthusiasm for heavy workouts, or incurred an injury. But when I consistently listen to my instincts, I make great progress in adding muscle mass and quality to my physique. When you become totally in tune with your body, you'll make great gains, avoid injuries, and always have great enthusiasm for your workouts.

While perusing the following routines, remember that I count neither sets nor reps, and I'm frequently even unaware of the weights I'm handling. I go totally by feel and continue blasting away at each body part until I feel that I have trained it as intensely as I could have on that particular day.

Here is a sample training program that I use during an off-season cycle:

DAY 1
(Back, Posterior Delts, Anterior Delts, Abdominals)

Narrow-grip Chins (with V-bar). Enough sets (probably 5–8 sets, although I've never actually counted them) taken to complete failure to fully exhaust my lats. Note: I place a stool beneath the bar and press down on it with my feet to boost my chest up to the bar for my pure negative reps. (For reference, my concept of total intensity was discussed earlier in this chapter, and it's further discussed in Chapter 5.)

Dumbbell Bent Laterals. Enough sets taken to complete failure to fully exhaust the posterior deltoids and upper-back muscles. Normally, I'll work up the rack and then back down the rack, going to failure on each down-the-rack set.

Cross-bench Dumbbell Pullovers. Enough sets taken to complete failure to fully exhaust the pectorals, latissimus dorsi, and serratus muscles.

Standing Machine Presses Behind Neck. Enough sets taken to complete failure to fully exhaust the anterior deltoids and triceps.

Deadlifts. (This movement is done only every other workout, as is explained in the notes at the end of this section.) Work up to two heavy sets of three reps, drop back to a light set of at least 10 reps, and sometimes jump the weight back up for another near-limit set of about three reps.

Note: Most exercises for muscle groups other than the abdominals are pyramided upwards, increasing the weight and decreasing the reps performed each set. Then I work back down in weight while doing progressively more reps each set; sometimes I will even work back up to a maximum weight again before terminating my exercise.

Roman Chair Sit-ups. I do 3–5 sets, each carried to the point where I can no longer forcefully contract my abdominals.

Incline Sit-ups. Same format as for Roman chair sit-ups.

Twists and/or Side Bends. Use no added resistance for 10–20 minutes nonstop.

Note: All workouts are concluded with a somewhat longer stretching session than was used in my preworkout warm-up. I stretch every joint and muscle group in my body after each workout, but I place greater concentration and time on stretching the body parts just trained.

DAY 2
(Chest, Medial Deltoids, Calves)

Note: I perform exercises for my posterior and anterior deltoid heads on a completely different day from my medial-delt workout, a practice that I've found places less wear and tear on my shoulder joints.

Dumbbell Incline Presses. I thoroughly warm up my shoulders and chest, then work up over five or six sets to my top weight (which is a pair of 180-pound dumbbells for five or six reps at the time of writing this book). Next, I quickly work back down in 30-pound increments, taking no rest between weight drops and

doing each weight-drop set to failure, plus usually past failure with forced reps.

Incline Dumbbell Flyes. Same procedure as for incline presses, except that I sometimes work back up the rack to the heaviest dumbbells I can handle after I've already gone up and down the rack one time.

Parallel Bar Dips. I do 3–5 sets close to failure, concentrating on stretching my pecs at the bottom of the movement and constantly *squeezing* my pectorals as intensely as possible throughout each repetition.

Standing Dumbbell Side Laterals. I do enough sets taken to complete failure to fully exhaust my medial delts (this could be in the range of 5–8 sets). On my side laterals, I'll frequently stop the weight in various positions and hold it for 5–10 seconds, statically contracting my medial delts for even greater intensity than I normally reach in a set.

Calf Machine Toe Raises. I do enough sets taken to complete failure to fully exhaust the gastrocnemius muscles of my calves (which is between 6–10 sets). I work up to a maximum poundage and then quickly make weight reductions, taking each weight-reduction set at least to failure and often past failure with forced reps. It's absolutely essential that you completely stretch your calves for a moment in the bottom position of each repetition and then rise up as high as possible on your toes.

DAY 3
(Arms and Abdominals)

Seated Dumbbell Curls. Take all sets to failure while working up and then back down the rack. Be sure to fully supinate your hands and wrists on each rep as you curl the dumbbells upwards, squeeze your biceps as tightly as you can at the top of the movement, then pronate your hands and wrists as you return the dumbbells back to the starting point. Your last two or three reps of each set should be performed as hammer curls, in which you curl the dumbbells and lower them with your thumbs up (i.e., with your palms facing towards each other throughout the movement).

Pulley Pushdowns. Start with a moderate weight to warm up your elbows, then work up and back down the rack in the usual manner. I finish off the exercise with a very heavy weight, doing as many half and quarter reps as I can handle.

Reverse-grip Dips. I do enough sets to exhaust my triceps, concentrating on the negative half of the movement by having my training partner push down on my shoulders as I mightily resist the extra force and am bulldozed downwards into the bottom position of the exercise.

Barbell Wrist Curls. This movement should be performed with palms up and forearms supported on a flat exercise bench. I do 3–5 sets with a very heavy weight and my partner pushes down on the bar to emphasize the negative cycle of the movement.

Do the same abdominal workout as on Day 1.

Look at Tom's excellent overall upper-body development as he reps out on wrist curls. (*Mike Neveux*)

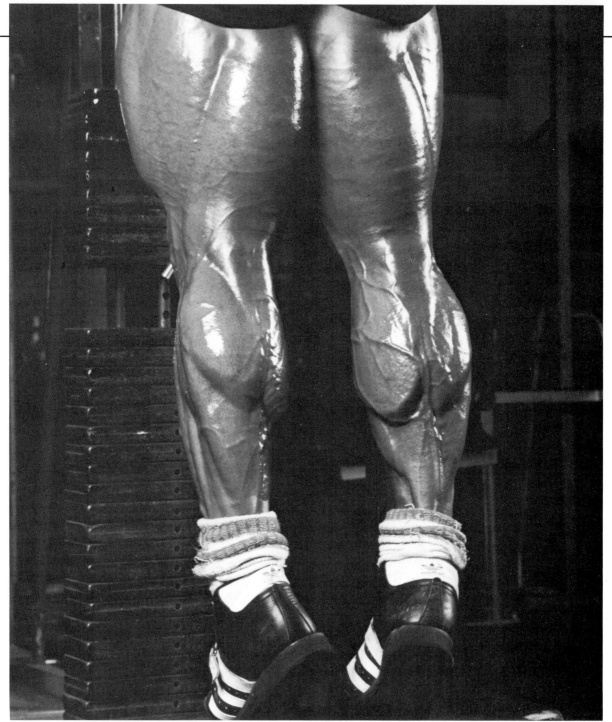

With thighs as huge and muscular as Tom's, his calves must be particularly well developed to look proportionate. (*John Balik*)

DAY 4 *(Thighs and Calves)*

Full Squats. After warming up thoroughly with stretches, free-hand squats, and several light, high-rep sets of squats, I work up over 4–6 sets to a heavy, fairly difficult set of 5–8 reps. I finish off with one moderate set of 30 reps, trying to do them all consecutively, without resting at all in the standing position between any of the repetitions.

Hack Squats. I work up with little rest between sets to a relatively hard set of 10–15 reps.

Leg Extensions. In this movement, I take all of my sets to failure while working up to a heavy weight (I probably do 5–8 total sets). I hold the top position of two or three reps per set for several seconds, squeezing my quadriceps muscles for all I'm worth, a technique that I feel helps me to achieve such deep cuts between my individual quadriceps muscles.

Leg Curls. I take all sets at least to failure while working up to a heavy weight (about 5–8 total sets are done). Occasionally, I'll have a training partner emphasize the negative cycle of a couple of reps at the end of several sets by pushing down on the lever arm of the machine to add resistance to the negative part of the repetition.

Standing Calf Machine Toe Raises. I do the same workout on the standing calf machine as I did on Day 2.

Seated Calf Machine Toe Raises. I do several sets of *very* heavy, low-rep toe raises to fully exhaust my soleus and gastrocnemius muscle groups. Even with the heaviest weights, however, I use a full range of motion and sometimes stop the weight for a ten-second static contraction in my calf muscles. Less frequently, I will use lighter weights, perform higher reps, but do the seated toe raise movement much more slowly over the full range of motion of the exercise.

Additional Workout Notes

1. After four workouts on my five-day cycle, I use my training instinct to evaluate my energy and workout enthusiasm levels, then decide to either rest a day or two before repeating my training cycle, or simply repeat the cycle without the rest day.

2. I tend to alternate cycles in which I train with absolutely maximum intensity with cycles in which I don't go quite as heavy, nor push as close to complete failure on each set.

3. I only do squats every other leg workout, but I still perform hack squats (but with a thorough warm-up before working up *and* down in weight), leg extensions, and leg curls on my non-squat leg workout days.

4. During a training cycle in which I plan to do squats, I drop deadlifts from my back routine; and during a workout cycle in which I don't plan to perform squats, I'll include deadlifts in my back program.

5. Heavy calf isometrics (statically holding a set position while contracting the calves) are done once in each series for every lower-leg exercise.

6. In order to shock my body with a radically new stress stimulus—thereby forcing it to grow stronger and more massive at a faster rate of speed—I often totally change a body part routine, or at least include an exercise in the training program that I haven't used in recent weeks or months.

7. Always remember this rule for off-season mass- and power-building workouts: *To build large, high-quality muscles, you must do low reps (4–6) in perfect form primarily on basic exercises.* Furthermore, you must not miss scheduled workouts, you must follow an effective musclebuilding diet (see Chapter 2), and you must maintain a positive mental attitude (see Chapter 8) at all times.

5 Precontest Training Tips

There are eleven methods presented in this chapter that you can use in conjunction with a low-calorie precontest diet to strip all superfluous fat from your body and noticeably harden up your physique for major bodybuilding championships. All of the great bodybuilders—such as Arnold Schwarzenegger, Lou Ferrigno, Dr. Franco Columbu, Frank Zane, Samir Bannout, and others whom you see gloriously depicted on the pages of *Muscle & Fitness*, *Flex*, *MuscleMag International*, and all of the other bodybuilding magazines—are religiously devoted to using these training principles and techniques to achieve the startling muscularity they display onstage at a competition.

It's amazing how radically the standard of bodybuilding in America has improved in recent years. Just since I entered my first Mr. America show in Philadelphia in 1976, standards have improved so much that the men winning state titles today are at least as good as a majority of national title winners during the early to mid-1970s. And I'd estimate that there are at least ten times the number of good bodybuilders today than when I broke into major competition. Why has this happened?

One of the foremost reasons for the gratifying explosion of popularity for bodybuilding is a result of the very favorable public-relations efforts of Arnold Schwarzenegger and Lou Ferrigno, and more recently of Rachel McLish. With all of the best bodybuilders presenting themselves so well on television talk shows, the public couldn't help but notice that we're not the muscleheads they thought we were. We're intelligent, articulate, well mannered, good-looking, polite, witty, and poised. As a result, there's been a massive flood of young men and women into bodybuilding, a sport that they would previously never have considered joining.

As shameful as it might be, greatly augmented use of anabolic steroids and other bodybuilding drugs has inevitably elevated the overall standard of bodybuilding. But with the IFBB initiating drug controls at major competitions beginning in 1984, your local physician and pharmacist will have less to do with the high standard of competitive bodybuilders. I believe that today's best bodybuilders would still be the best even if it were impossible to obtain and use anabolic agents. Steroids don't make champions; you make yourself a champion.

Improved knowledge of nutrition and the principles of the sport are also responsible to a degree for today's great physiques. At my first few national competitions, I followed a low-carbohydrate diet, which flattened out my physique and made me feel incredibly miserable. But today I have been able to retain a great deal of mass while getting ripped to shreds using a low-fat/high-carbohydrate diet. And as I have, hundreds of aspiring bodybuilders have learned to use their minds to dramatically improve their physiques.

This brings me to one of the primary reasons why today's champion bodybuilders look like the Farnese Hercules come to life. There's been an incredible leap forward in understanding all of the training methods that combine to develop a bodybuilding champ, and this information has been widely disseminated across America and the rest of the world. Even a kid who lives in a town of only 200 citizens can become a functional expert on bodybuilding techniques if he at least subscribes to *Muscle & Fitness* magazine and purchases certain key bodybuilding books.

While individual bodies react differently to each distinct training and dietary stimulus, there are certain principles that are universally applicable to all healthy, reasonably athletic men and women. Therefore, I can tell you the best type of precontest diet for your body type and metabolic rate, explain the precontest training strategies in this chapter clearly enough for you to fully understand them, and with no additional coaching you can achieve excellent competitive condition the first time out of the gate. Granted, you might not peak 100 percent on the exact day of your competition because you need to peak out for a competition three or four times before you can get the timing of a peak mastered. Still, you can achieve an incredible physique without actually having a coach.

So with my long—but I feel important—preamble out of the way, we will discuss the following eleven precontest training topics in this chapter: Quality Training; Aerobics and Bodybuilding; Trisets and Giant Sets; Peak Contraction; Continuous Tension; Burns; the Stripping Method; Negative Reps; Rest-Pause Training; my own concept of Maximum Training Intensity (Extended Sets Training); Double-Split Routines.

Quality Training

There are three primary ways in which you can increase workout intensity:

1. Do a greater number of reps with a specific weight.
2. Do the same number of reps with a heavier weight.
3. Do the same number of sets and reps with a consistent training poundage, but progressively reduce the length of rest intervals between sets.

In regular off-season training, you will use a combination of the first two methods to increase intensity. However, when you are peaking for a competition, you will use the third method of increasing workout intensity. And this technique of progressively shortening rest intervals between sets is called *quality training*.

The mind plays a key role in quality training. The weight doesn't make the muscles grow; your mind does. Keep mentally focussed even when you're training quickly.

When you try to quality-train with low-energy reserves—as is the case when you are following a precontest diet—you will find it impossible to continue working out with the same heavy weights as you used in the off-season. Therefore, a reduction of 50 percent in your workout poundages can be expected when quality training. But as long as you are still lifting the heaviest possible training weights, quality training and a strict precontest diet will help you to achieve an incredible degree of muscularity for a competition.

In my own case—as well as in my observations of most of the other superstar bodybuilders who train in California—very few of the top people actually quality-train prior to a competition. Rather than reducing the length of rest intervals between sets, they will make each set more intense. At best, I'll start a precontest set only slightly before I feel fully recuperated from my previous all-out, high-intensity set.

This may sound somewhat contradictory, but it doesn't matter that much how I train or diet for a major competition. Usually the mere thought of an up-

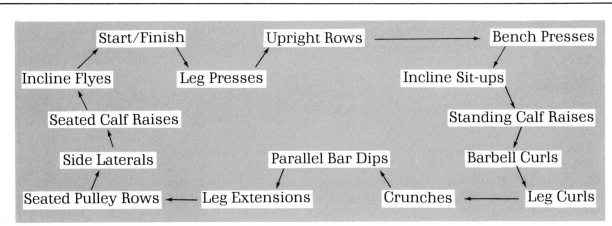

Figure 5–1: Circuit Training Program

coming show and my visualization of how I intend to look onstage at that event makes me peak regardless of how I train and eat. The mind really *is* that powerful.

Circuit Training

With experimentation, you may well discover that you must follow a quality-training strategy in order to reach an optimum peak in which you combine both mass and muscularity. One of the easiest and most enjoyable ways of quality training is to circuit-train. You can highly recommend circuit training to fitness enthusiasts who wish to develop cardio-respiratory condition, strength, and a muscular physique through only one form of physical activity.

In circuit training you will set up a series of 15–20 exercises around a gym covering all parts of your body. No two consecutive exercise stations should include movements for the same part of the body, however. Once you have set up your circuit, you can move from one exercise to the next, resting no more time than is required to walk from one station to the next. At first this will be exceedingly fatiguing, but your body will quickly become used to it and you'll be able to comfortably do 3–5 trips through your circuit for a full-body workout.

You will find a sample circuit-training program in Figure 5–1 above. Do 8–12 reps of each exercise, except abdominal movements in which you can perform 25–30 reps.

PHA Training

PHA (an abbreviation for Peripheral Heart Action) training is a variation of circuit training in which you do shorter circuits of four to six exercises each. This method was popularized by Dr. Bob Gajda, who won the Mr. America and Mr. Universe titles in the mid-1960s. PHA training enjoyed a brief vogue, but then fell out of popularity, which is unfortunate because it is an excellent system of training.

In Gajda's system, exercises for all parts of the body were assembled into circuits of only four to six movements, and each of these short circuits was repeated several times. Exercises were chosen so you would be forced to skip from body part to body part, and in the end bodybuilders who followed the PHA system were able to do tremendous numbers of total sets with relatively little fatigue buildup, giving them an excellent quality of muscular development.

A sample PHA program that you can use three nonconsecutive days per week is outlined in Figure 5–2 on page 96. Do

8–12 repetitions of each exercise (20–30 reps on abdominal movements), and repeat every circuit three to five times before moving on to the next one. Finally, be sure to begin PHA training slowly, perhaps doing only one cycle of each short circuit the initial workout, then building up intensity in gradual increments from that starting point.

Aerobics and Bodybuilding

Aerobic training in addition to bodybuilding workouts is absolutely essential during a peaking cycle in order to metabolize stored body fat. Indeed, the three key factors that have resulted in the most massive and ripped-up physiques of today are heavy, high-intensity bodybuilding training, a low-fat diet, and plenty of aerobic exercise.

Physiologically, the anaerobic training of a heavy-weight workout doesn't burn up body fat. Instead, it uses glycogen (carbohydrates) stored in the muscles, blood stream, and liver for its source of fuel. But in long-lasting, low-intensity aerobic training, your body primarily burns stored fat to provide its energy needs.

Cycling along the beach is my favorite form of aerobic activity during a peaking cycle. I prefer cycling because it places a lot less stress on the leg joints than running. Swimming is also an excellent form of aerobic training, and it places even less stress on the leg joints than cycling. And if you enjoy watching sweaty, happy women and men, you could even occasionally take an organized aerobic exercise class.

One thing you need to understand about aerobic training is that its intensity and duration are cycled from off-season to precontest phases, the same way diet and weight workouts are cycled. As I increase my fat consumption after a competition, the amount of aerobics I perform is drastically reduced. Perhaps I will do only one or two half-hour aerobic sessions in the off-season, versus one or two hours of aerobic workouts *daily* prior to competing. And when I

Figure 5–2: PHA Training Program

Series I	Series II	Series III
Squats	Military Presses	Hyperextensions
Incline Presses	Leg Extensions	Side Laterals
Barbell Wrist Curls	Barbell Curls	Leg Curls
Seated Pulley Rows	Parallel Bar Dips	Upright Rows
Front Raises	Calf Presses	Lying Triceps Extensions
Pulley Pushdowns	Front Lat Pulldowns	
Series IV	**Series V**	**Series VI**
Pec-Deck Flyes	Leg Presses	Concentration Curls
Reverse Curls	Cable Crossovers	Incline Sit-ups
Seated Calf Raises	Reverse Wrist Curls	Standing Calf Raises
Hanging Leg Raises	Crunches	Stiff-legged Deadlifts
Pulldowns Behind Neck		

Note: Rest minimally between exercises and only 60–90 seconds between cycles.

keep my threshold of aerobic training low in the off-season, I seem to get an enhanced fat-burning effect from it once I boost my aerobics up to a high level.

It's important to understand that even though you might have a basic training plan to follow, it's acceptable to change it from day to day according to your changing analysis of your needs. Sometimes you have to get out of shape in order to reach a new peak of condition. No bodybuilder or other athlete can maintain a peak level of performance indefinitely, so you must cycle your bodybuilding training, aerobics, and diet accordingly.

Trisets and Giant Sets

Trisets are groups of three exercises performed with no rest between movements and a normal rest interval between trisets. Giant sets are groups of four to six exercises done with no rest interval between them and a somewhat longer-than-normal interval between giant sets. Both trisets and giant sets are good ways to inject new stimuli into your training, which gives you better results from your workouts.

I lose my ability to concentrate on each movement when I jump from exercise to exercise, although many other top bodybuilders can accomplish this task quite well. Most of my training is done with straight sets, although I've had good success in supersetting one heavy movement for a particular body part with a lighter exercise for the same muscle group. For example, I can stimulate my pectorals with great intensity by supersetting dumbbell incline presses with flat-bench flyes.

If you decide to give trisets a trial in your workouts, it's best to do them for larger, multi-faceted muscle groups like your back, thighs, chest, or deltoids. The following are sample trisets for each of these four body parts:

BACK

1. Shrugs (trapezius)
2. Seated Pulley Rows (latissimus dorsi)
3. Hyperextensions (erector spinae)

THIGHS

1. Leg Presses (quadriceps mass)
2. Leg Curls (hamstrings)
3. Leg Extensions (quadriceps shape)

CHEST

1. Incline Presses (upper pectorals)
2. Pec-deck Flyes (inner-outer pectorals)
3. Cross-bench Pullovers (pectoral-serratus tie-ins)

DELTOIDS

1. Presses Behind Neck (anterior deltoids)
2. Side Laterals (medial deltoids)
3. Bent Laterals (posterior deltoids)

Giant sets are best performed for large antagonistic body parts like the chest and back. The following is a sample six-exercise giant set for your chest and back:

1. Incline Dumbbell Presses (upper pecs)
2. Chins (lat width)
3. Bench Presses (lower/outer pecs)
4. Seated Pulley Rows (lat width/ thickness)
5. Cable Crossovers (pec shape/ cuts)
6. T-bar Rows (lat thickness)

You'll recover faster between giant sets if you spend your rest interval stretching the muscles being trained. I firmly believe in stretching before, after, and even during a workout. Stretching your muscles and connective tissues will help prevent injuries and develop greater muscle contractile ability.

Keep in mind that your training increases in intensity according to how many exercises you compound in your workout. Supersets are of much higher intensity than straight sets. By increasing the degree of intensity, you will have trisets, four-exercise, five-exercise, and six-exercise giant sets.

Peak Contraction

The more completely contracted a muscle is, the more individual muscle cells contracted (shortened); the more muscle cells contracted, the greater is the potential for development if you place a heavy weight on the working muscles.

To understand the preceding statement, you need to know something about the physiology of muscle contraction. The most basic unit of a muscle is a muscle cell, and hundreds of muscle cells are joined end to end to form muscle fibres. Bundles of fibres form skeletal muscles. And a muscle cell will either contract completely or not at all when a skeletal muscle is under a load. There are no half contractions of muscle cells.

Obviously, you should have a maximum weight on each muscle when it has been optimally shortened. But it's unfortunate that many exercises don't allow such a peak contraction effect. As much as I believe in doing squats, the weight is supported on a column of bone and there is little quad contraction in the end position of the movement.

To put peak contraction on your quads, you would need to do leg extensions, in which your quads bear a very heavy weight in the completely contracted position. Most machine exercises give you a peak contraction effect,

as do concentration curls, dumbbell kickbacks, barbell rows, shrugs, hyperextensions, and many other exercises.

It's important to note that you can also apply a peak contraction effect to a muscle by mentally willing it. For example, you can feel a peak contraction in your quads at the top of a squat movement if you consciously tense your quadriceps muscles as hard as possible when your legs are straight. Your progress in bodybuilding depends on the mind and how well you use it to improve the quality of muscle contraction on each rep of every exercise.

Continuous Tension

Doing a slow, full-range movement with continuous tension to the working muscles is often very important to me. When you do a short repetition, or let momentum move the bar part of the way along its exercise range, you often lose much of the resistance you should feel in your muscles. And there can be no doubt that feeling maximum resistance in each exercise is one of the biggest secrets of bodybuilding success.

One way to keep continuous tension on your muscles is to do nonlock movements. An example of this would be coming up to within six inches of a straight-leg position in squats, then immediately going back down to the bottom point of the movement. You can actually rest your thigh muscles when your legs are straight during a set of squats. The same can be said for many other exercises in which you can rest when your arms and/or legs are straight.

I'll often build up a maximum intensity contraction by holding a weight in the start or end position of an exercise, contracting the muscles as hard as possible before continuing the movement. Many bodybuilders rest in this—or some other—position in an exercise, which is a grave mistake in terms of failing to place maximum stress on a working body part.

technique of Arnold Schwarzenegger. It is much like doing forced reps, and it can also be compared with circuit training done with a single exercise.

One good feature of Tom's regular training style is the extreme range of motion he gets in each exercise, as in this set of incline flyes. (*Mike Neveux*)

Burns

I probably think more about burns (short, partial movements in an exercise) and tension in my muscles than about anything else each workout. I use burns and tension to build up the pain, then put it out of my mind and build it up even higher. When I can't do any more full reps, I'll do half or partial reps, which defines burns for me. Or I'll hold a weight, as described in the preceding section on continuous tension.

The Stripping Method

Stripping (sometimes called *descending sets*) is a favorite training-intensification

In Chapter 1, I explained how you can use forced reps to push your muscles to continue working well past the point of brief muscular failure by having your training partner assist you by pulling up on the bar. With descending sets, you actually reduce the weight as you reach the failure point in an exercise, which also allows you to forge past failure and into a much more productive muscle-growth zone.

To first use the stripping method, let's say that you're going to perform descending sets on your bench presses. First take a good warm-up, then load up the bar with plenty of small plates, matching the load configurations on each side and leaving the collars off the bar. Load on enough weight to restrict yourself to five or six strict reps to failure, then lie down on the bench and go to failure in good form. Don't place the bar back on the rack; ask training partners stationed at each end of the bar to simultaneously remove 10–20 pounds from each side of the barbell. With this weight drop accomplished, you grind out three or four more reps, have another weight drop, and finally force out your last supertough three or four reps.

His entire body gets into the act as Tom forces out rep after rep of leg extensions. Look at that massive lat poking out behind his right arm! (Mike Neveux)

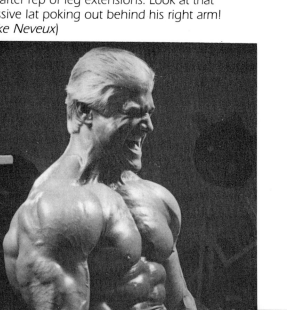

If you don't have training partners available, you can still use the stripping method with most dumbbell exercises by simply going down the rack in a movement. For example, you can start a descending set of dumbbell presses by using a pair of 60s for five or six good reps, then immediately a pair of 55s for three or four reps, a pair of 50s for three or four counts, and perhaps a final set of three or four with a pair of 45s. This will be exceedingly painful, but the procedure builds huge, high-quality muscles! There's always an element of pain that must be overcome if you want a superstar physique.

Negative Reps

Everyone who's serious about bodybuilding has by now heard about negative reps. I definitely like to place extra stress on the negative (downward) movement of an exercise, and I think that bodybuilders have been doing this since the days of Sandow. The easiest way to emphasize the negative part of a rep is to slowly lower the weight each time, feeling the continuous tension on the way down in a movement. As a rule of thumb, take about twice as long to lower the weight than to raise it, and you're on the right track.

A more intense form of negative stress can be found in the technique called *forced negative reps*. With this training principle, your workout partner will push down on the weight and add to the resistance that you feel as you are lowering back to the starting point. You raise the weight on your own, then lower the increased resistance. Or even more intensely, you allow your partner to give you a bit of a forced rep, then resist his forced negative as you return to the starting position.

I believe that it's unreasonable to expect a couple of training partners to give you pure negative reps in which they raise a very heavy weight up for you, then let you lower it back to the starting point while mightily resisting its downward momentum. No training partner is going to willingly sacrifice his training time and energies to help you every day with such a technique, so it's better for you to learn how to emphasize the negative part of a movement either on your own or with the assistance of a single training partner.

Rest-Pause Training

Like all serious bodybuilders, I'm always looking for new ways in which to intensify my training sessions, and rest-pause workouts provide an excellent method for this. However, I don't feel that you should rush into using this technique, which ultimately allows you to use heavier work loads. And when you start to burn out on this method, which is easy to do, switch off to some other technique of training intensification.

What is rest-pause training? In its most basic form, it's a way in which you can severely overload a working muscle group with an absolute maximum amount of weight for relatively high reps in each exercise. And as you no doubt already understand, the greater the overload you place on your muscles, the more they must respond to this by growing in mass and strength.

The problem with using heavy weights in a workout is that you can only handle them for two or three reps in optimum form. A good bodybuilding set consists of 8–12 reps, so you need to develop a method by which you can do this higher number of reps in a set with absolutely the maximum amount of weight.

The key to rest-pause training lies in the fact that you can recuperate more than 50 percent of a muscle's strength and endurance with just 10–15 seconds of rest. So the idea is to first warm up completely, then load the bar with a weight that restricts you to no more than three reps performed in strict form. Do these three reps, put the weight down, rest 10–15 seconds, pick the weight up, and do another one or two reps. At this point, you will usually need to make a very quick reduction in the amount of weight you're handling, but it has to be quick enough to allow you to again pick up the bar 15 seconds later for two or three additional reps. Finally, you finish off your rest-pause set by taking a final rest-pause and grinding out your last reps.

You *must* use basic exercises (e.g., the squat, bench press, and seated pulley row) in your rest-pause training, and you should do a rest-pause workout for each muscle group no more frequently than once every two weeks. In my experience, using rest-pause workouts too often or on the wrong exercises will hold back your progress. And, again, don't rush into rest-pause work until you have many months of steady, high-intensity training in your workout diary.

When you've already blasted your pectorals and deltoids to the limit with bench presses, inclines, and flat-bench flyes, just one or two sets of parallel bar dips can make a strong man cry out in anguish. (*Mike Neveux*)

Maximum Training

Maximum training intensity is a relative concept. From one workout to the next, you will find yourself able to put either greater or lesser effort into each set, even though you might very well be putting out 100 percent effort in every workout. These fluctuations are a result of several factors, most notably how well you are concentrating on your workouts each day. Other factors that have a bearing on how hard you are pumping iron are your eating habits, amount of sleep, how completely you are able to recuperate between workouts, and the presence or absence of chronic injuries.

The key to achieving maximum intensity each training session is to ask yourself the question, "Am I training as hard as I mentally and physically can, given my present attitude towards my workouts?" The answer may depend on the unbroken stream of forced reps, descending sets, cheating reps, rest-pause sets, and so forth that make each workout of maximum intensity. Never settle for second best in terms of training intensity, or you will have no hope of becoming a champion bodybuilder.

Double-Split Routines

A double-split routine consists of two training sessions per day, one in the morning and the other in the late afternoon or early evening, a program that is maintained six days per week. However, I prefer to do most of my heavy weight work in the mornings and have my evenings free for only abdominal and/or aerobic training. When I go on a full double-split routine, I tend to burn out in two weeks and end up thinking that I'll hate bodybuilding for the rest of my life.

The most basic form of double-split routine involves a heavy session in the morning for your larger muscle groups, followed by a nightly workout for only your abs, calves, and/or forearms. Or you can work with a system in which you train twice a day three days per week and only once on three other days. The following is an example of this modified double-split routine:

Monday-Wednesday-Friday

(A.M.)
Abdominals
Chest
Back

(P.M.)
Calves
Shoulders
Upper Arms

Tuesday-Thursday-Saturday

(A.M. or P.M.)
Abs and/or Calves
Thighs
Forearms

A full double-split routine, consisting of two major workouts per day, six days a week, is of exceedingly high intensity, and very few bodybuilders will be able to tolerate one. The following is an example of how you would set up a full double-split routine:

Monday-Wednesday-Friday

(A.M.)
Abdominals
Thighs
Forearms

(P.M.)
Calves (heavy)
Back
Biceps

Tuesday-Thursday-Saturday

(A.M.)
Abdominals
Chest
Neck

(P.M.)
Calves (light)
Shoulders
Triceps

One primary advantage to training more frequently each day is the fact that you need not totally exhaust your energy reserves in each training session, as is the case when you take one long, daily workout. Another positive factor is the beneficial effect frequent workouts have on your metabolism. The more often you train each day—whether these sessions are weight workouts or aerobic sessions—the faster your metabolism will become and the easier it will be for you to get completely ripped up the last three weeks before a competition.

Optimum Physical Condition

One by-product of hard bodybuilding training is the incredible physical condition you achieve as a result of it, and I feel that more athletes should consider using high-intensity bodybuilding methods to get back into peak shape for sports participation. The hard anaerobic and aerobic training you do is coupled with a low-calorie diet to increase muscle mass, decrease body fat, improve strength, increase flexibility, and even advance your degree of cardio-respiratory fitness. And this puts you in tremendous shape to get the most out of your hard-won athletic skills.

Definites do not exist in bodybuilding. No one can tell you exactly what to do, so you have to determine what's best for yourself through self-experimentation.

So many people are concerned with numbers these days. But I think a good bodybuilder should get more into how a working muscle *feels*. Sets and reps are fine, but what does it *feel* like to have your biceps expand to massive measurements? What did you do mentally to set this up?

Because I am a *feeler* rather than a *lifter*, I'm giving you fewer numbers and more ways to identify feelings in this book. Believe me, you'll get more out of your training when you reach the advanced state of being a sense-oriented bodybuilder.

6 Diet for the Competitive Edge

Assuming that your mental approach is optimum, off-season bodybuilding is about 50 percent training and 50 percent diet. During the last six to eight weeks prior to a competition, however, diet can be as much as 80 percent of the battle. Therefore, the subject of precontest diet is of paramount importance to all competitive bodybuilders.

In this chapter, I will discuss the following topics: low-fat diet; low-carbohydrate diet; precontest supplementation; the revolutionary new cytotoxic diet; and my own precontest dietary strategy.

Low-Fat Diet

One of the main reasons why today's superstar bodybuilders are able to maintain such an incredible amount of muscle mass while getting completely cut up for a competition is the advent of the high-carbohydrate/low-fat diet. The classic precontest bodybuilding diet previously was a high-fat/low-carbohydrate menu, which definitely gets a bodybuilder ripped up, but which cannot possibly allow you to maintain great muscle mass while dieting down. Beginning in the mid-1970s, bodybuilders flocked en masse to low-fat dieting, and the gold rush to supermuscular physiques was on!

It's a scientific certainty that by consuming less calories you gradually reduce body fat. And reducing body fat to a very low level is what it's all about just prior to a competition.

It's equally certain that following a low-fat diet is the easiest way to create a caloric deficit. And while on a low-fat/low-calorie regimen, you can follow a healthy, balanced diet high in fresh vegetables and fruit. Low-carb diets are very poorly balanced—and thus unhealthy—because they are virtually devoid of fruit and veggies.

Fats are the most concentrated forms of energy in your diet, more than twice as rich a source of calories as either protein or carbohydrates. One gram of fat yields about nine calories when metabolized within your body for energy. In contrast, both protein and carbohydrate yield approximately four calories per gram. Therefore, it's only logical that your diet will be lower in calories if you strictly reduce your intake of fat, replacing fats with either protein or carbohydrates.

Virtually all animal-source foods are high in fats. These foods include pork, beef, whole milk and its by-products, and eggs. Other high-fat foods include nuts, seeds, corn, and avocados. Meats low in fat include most fish and poultry without the fatty skin. Fruit and most vegetables are quite low in fat content.

In order to scientifically conduct a low-fat diet, you must first determine your caloric maintenance level by keeping a dietary journal for a full week during which you neither gain nor lose weight. Add up all of the calories you consume that week, divide by seven, and you will have an accurate figure for a daily caloric maintenance level.

You can get a more approximate figure by multiplying your body weight in pounds by 19. Using this formula, a 200-pound bodybuilder would have a daily caloric maintenance level of 3800 calories. In the absence of a one-week dietary record when not gaining or losing weight, this simple formula will give you a figure for caloric maintenance to use with a low-fat/low-calorie diet.

Once you have determined your caloric maintenance level, you can begin a low-fat diet by consuming about 200 less calories per day than your maintenance figure. And each week on your diet, you should progressively reduce your caloric intake by about 200 additional calories. In the end, you may go as low as 1200–1500 calories per day, but you probably won't need to go under 2000 calories per day, as long as you do plenty of aerobics and are willing to spend at least two months on a moderate diet.

The following is a sample low-fat/low-calorie precontest diet that you can give a trial in your own competition preparation:

> **Breakfast**. Egg whites, bran cereal with skim milk, supplements, coffee.
>
> **Lunch**. Tuna salad with a minimum of dressing, fruit, rice, supplements, iced tea.
>
> **Dinner**. Broiled fish, baked potato, green vegetable, supplements, coffee.
>
> **Snacks**. Whole-grain toast (dry), popcorn (dry), fresh fruit.

The length of time you spend dieting for a competition depends on how out of shape you allowed yourself to get in the off-season, how strictly you wish to diet, and how much aerobic training you do. I'd suggest starting your first diet six to eight weeks before your show, making sure to take good written and photographic notes of your progress and the variables that contributed to each change in your physical appearance.

The first time you diet, it's essential that you keep a record of how many calories you consume at each meal. After one or two peaks, however, you can begin to use your training instinct (discussed in Chapter 10). I follow such an instinctive approach, gearing the severity of my diet and aerobic training according to how long I have left before my competition and how trim I look in the mirror.

The following are ten low-fat dieting hints that will help you to get ripped up for your next competition:

1. **Never fry foods**. All main dishes should be broiled, baked, or boiled. If you do fry foods, use a non-stick skillet sprayed with a bit of Pam. Fried foods soak up high-calorie oils like sponges, greatly increasing the caloric content of the food.

2. **Choose low-fat meats**. If you can make a choice between beef and pork, choose beef, which has a lower fat content, and hence a lower caloric content. Similarly, choose poultry over red meat and fish over poultry for your main dishes.

3. **Consume nonfat milk products**. If you must consume milk and milk products, be sure to use the nonfat variety. Similarly, you should not consume the high-fat yolks of the eggs. Many bodybuilders should avoid milk completely for the last two or three weeks before a show to avoid retaining excess water.

4. **Steam your veggies**. Most bodybuilders boil their vegetables, a cooking process which destroys many of the vitamins and minerals contained in the veggies. After lightly steaming your vegetables, be sure to avoid putting butter or oil on them.

5. **Avoid sodium**. Sodium intake has nothing to do with the fat content of your diet, but sodium does retain enormous quantities

of water in your body. Avoid consuming table salt, salted foods, diet drinks (which are high in sodium), and such high-sodium foods as celery.

6. **Avoid oily salad dressings**. Use vinegar and/or lemon juice on your salads rather than oil and vinegar or other oil-containing dressings. It's possible to consume a very high number of calories just in the dressings you put on salad.

7. **Avoid butter**. Eat baked potatoes, popcorn, and bread without butter or margarine. These foods aren't high in calories, but the toppings you put on them are.

8. **Use herbs and spices**. You can make even dry chicken into a taste treat by cooking with herbs and spices. They can also spice up the remainder of any low-calorie meal.

9. **Eat low-fat breads**. Buy bread that has been baked with a minimum of high-fat butter or other oils, usually found in health-food stores. You should use it instead of other breads cooked with extra fats.

10. **Eat naturally sweet fruits**. Whenever you have a craving for junk foods, you can assuage it with a serving of high-sugar fruit, such as melon or strawberries.

Low-Carbohydrate Diet

Although most competitive bodybuilders follow low-fat/low-calorie diets prior to a competition, there are still some advocates of high-fat/low-carbohydrate dieting. Low-carb diets are particularly popular among naturally thin bodybuilders who usually have great difficulty in gaining muscular bodyweight. Using a low-fat diet, they often tend to flatten out and lose muscle mass; on a low-carbohydrate diet, they can get ripped to shreds without losing as much mass, because they can consume more fat.

A low-carb diet definitely works, particularly when you seek to eliminate all excess body water. Each gram of carbohydrate in your system holds four grams of water in your body, so eliminating or severely restricting carbohydrate consumption minimizes the amount of water retained in your body.

Even though natural ectomorphs can retain more muscle mass on a low-carbohydrate diet, most other bodybuilders tend to lose too much size on such a diet. In 1977, I restricted my carbohydrate consumption for the Mr. America contest, and I feel that I lost at least 20 pounds of solid muscle mass on the diet. I was cut, but I was incredibly small.

You should experiment with a low-carb diet in order to determine how well it works for you. I never felt comfortable on a low-carbohydrate diet. My energy levels were always low, and I frequently felt irritable and out of sorts. Switching to a low-fat/low-calorie diet solved all of these problems for me, but you still might benefit from adhering to a low-carb diet.

All you'll need to correctly follow a low-carb diet is an inexpensive carbohydrate booklet that you can find in pharmacies and health-food stores. This booklet will list the number of grams of carbohydrate for each serving of virtually any food that you might wish to eat. And you'll find that all types of meat, poultry, fish, eggs, hard cheese, and salad are extremely low in carbohydrate content.

Begin your low-carbohydrate diet by initially limiting carbohydrate consumption to approximately 150 grams per day for one week. Each succeeding week, you should reduce your carbohydrate consumption by 20–30 additional grams, working down to a minimum level of about 30 grams per day. *Do not under any circumstances attempt to reduce your carbohydrate consumption to zero because such a practice is very hard on your body.*

The following is a sample low-carb diet for use prior to a competition:

Breakfast. Eggs fried in butter, bacon, one-half cantaloupe, supplements, tea.

Lunch. Broiled chicken, hard cheese, green salad with oil-and-vinegar dressing, supplements, tea.

Dinner. Steak, green beans, supplements, coffee.

Snacks. Ham, cold beef, cold chicken, hard cheese.

As you can easily see, a low-carbohydrate diet can be very high in fat content and still be effective. And because of the high-fat intake, you will seldom become hungry when following this diet.

Precontest Supplementation

I get a much better boost from higher precontest supplementation when my off-season thresholds have been maintained at a minimum level. Prior to a major competition, I will take approximately five times as many supplements as I consume during the off-season. I actually end up taking vitamins and minerals at each meal, rather than just with my main early meal in the off-season.

Prior to a competition, I recommend that you take two or three multipacks of vitamins, minerals, and trace elements per day, always with meals in order to promote optimum assimilation of the nutrients. This minimum level of food supplementation will ensure maintenance of a high degree of health, which in turn makes it possible for you to get the most out of your training.

I also believe you should take extra water-soluble vitamins and electrolyte minerals. The water-soluble vitamins are B complex and C. And the electrolyte minerals are potassium, calcium, and magnesium. You can purchase special tablets that combine all three electrolytes at health-food stores.

Electrolytes are released from your body by way of perspiration, causing a sensation of great fatigue if you fail to regularly replace them. Obviously, you would find it difficult to train at peak efficiency and intensity if you constantly felt deeply fatigued. Therefore, it's absolutely essential that you take electrolytes prior to a competition, if not also during an off-season training cycle.

Another precontest supplement that you can experiment with is desiccated liver tablets. I've never noticed that much difference in my energy levels when I'm taking up to 100 liver tablets per day, but many other top bodybuilders have noticed greatly increased energy reserves when taking at least 30 tablets per day. Use your training instinct to determine if it works for you.

Cytotoxic Diet

If you have a great deal of difficulty with water retention prior to a competition—as well as during the off-season—you should investigate the new cytotoxic diet. It appears to show promise as a diet that results in minimum water retention.

Cyto means "cell" and *toxic* means "capable of killing." And the theory behind cytotoxic dieting is that certain foods in a bodybuilder's diet are allergenic and can kill cells. The result of a cytotoxic allergy to certain foods is inflammations within your body, such as tendinitis and mild arthritis. In turn, inflammations retain water as part of your body's attempt to heal these maladies.

By eliminating allergenic foods from your diet, you can reduce or completely heal these body inflammations and thus eliminate water-retention problems.

The best way to determine allergenic foods is to take an actual cytotoxic test administered by physicians specializing in allergy treatments and/or internal medicine. In this test, a sample of your blood is centrifuged to remove the white blood cells, which are then placed on microscope slides with a wide variety of food concentrates. Cells that have been distorted or destroyed by a food are clear proof that you are allergic to it. You may be allergic to 20–50 foods.

If you can't afford a cytotoxic test or are unable to find a physician to give it to you, you can eliminate certain foods to which 90 to 95 percent of all men and women have an allergic reaction. These foods are refined sugar (which most bodybuilders avoid anyway during a precontest cycle), milk and milk products, and grains other than rice. Merely curtailing your intake of these things for two weeks will greatly reduce water retention if you are allergic to certain foods.

Tom Platz's Precontest Diet

The severity of my precontest diet depends on my particular condition and how many weeks I have remaining until my competition. I have firmly established weekly checkpoints—daily for the last couple of weeks—for how I should look at various stages leading up to a Mr. Olympia contest. If I'm behind schedule (i.e., I'm not cutting up quickly enough), I will reduce my caloric consumption a bit and increase the amount of aerobic training I do. If I'm ahead of schedule, I'll initially try raising my calorie/carbohydrate consumption and reducing my aerobics. And if I'm drastically ahead of schedule, I'll increase my fat consumption, although this is always a last-ditch extreme.

I normally consume protein only twice per day during a peaking cycle, although I will sometimes eat protein three or four times per day when I sense that I'm not consuming enough of this musclebuilding nutrient. I'll take my vitamin and mineral supplements before each of four meals per day.

Preworkout Meal. Two pieces of toast with jelly, hot cereal, small glass of juice.

Postworkout Meal. Water-packed tuna (perhaps with a little mustard or relish on it), plain bagel, iced tea.

Snack. (two hours after second meal). Bagel and an apple.

Snack (again, two hours later). Two pieces of toast and half a grapefruit.

Evening Meal (about 8:30 P.M.). Plain, boiled fish, dry baked potato, salad with lemon slices, perhaps a steamed vegetable, water or a glass of dry white wine.

Compared to other precontest nutritional programs, this is definitely a no-frills diet. But all of my programs are similarly simple and devoid of fancy embellishments. I don't think that high-level bodybuilding is a very complicated process. Stick to the basics, and you'll come out ahead in the long run with a minimum of confusion.

7 Precontest Exercises & Routines

There are 21 exercises fully described and illustrated in this chapter. Added to the 20 movements that you learned to correctly perform in Chapter 4, you will have a sufficient pool of bodybuilding exercises for both off-season and precontest training at any ability level. Although I'm calling the exercises in this chapter "precontest" movements, you can use many of them during both off-season and precontest workout cycles. However, most of these exercises are used by bodybuilders primarily prior to a competition.

After you learn my methods of performing these 21 advanced-level exercises, I'll give you two progressively more difficult training programs that you can put to good use, and then describe how I train during a peaking cycle. If you sequentially follow the training programs suggested in Chapter 4 and then the routines outlined in this chapter, you'll take giant steps towards building a winning physique!

Your goal during a peaking cycle should be to strip away all excess body fat to reveal the hard-earned muscle mass that you have built up during your off-season cycle. However, you won't be able to improve the contour and overall development of a weak muscle group during a precontest cycle; that can only be accomplished during the off-season.

It takes a three-pronged attack to reach peak condition: training, diet, and mental approach. Each of these three factors is like the leg of a tripod, which cannot stand if a leg is missing. Therefore, you must pay careful attention to each factor in order to reach an optimum peak.

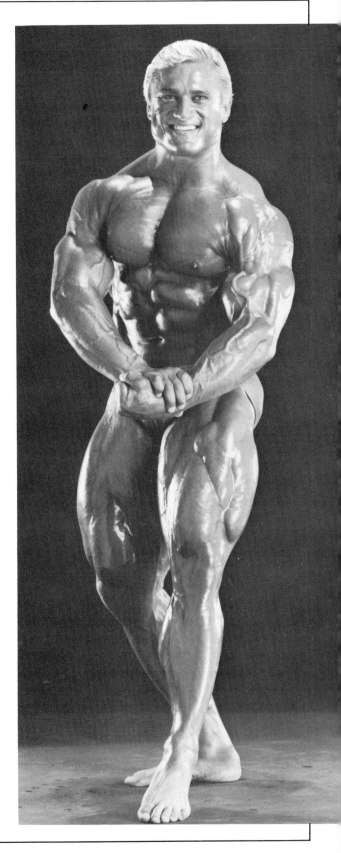

Hack Squats

Start

Values. Hack squats are a very good quadriceps isolation movement, particularly for the muscles just above the knees and the outer sections of the quads, which give your thighs a long, aesthetic muscle sweep.

Starting Point. There are two types of hack machines. With the yoke-type machine, position your shoulders under the yokes, bend your legs enough to position your feet with your heels together and toes angled outward at 45-degree angles, then straighten your legs. Finally, rotate the stop bars near your shoulders to release the weight carriage for use. With the sliding-platform version of a hack machine, first place your feet with your heels close together and toes angled outward at 45-degree angles. Bend your legs fully, place your back flat against the movable platform, and grasp the handles near the bottom of the platform. Straighten your legs, and you're ready to do the exercise.

Movement Performance. Slowly bend your legs as much as possible, being sure that your knees travel outward directly over your toes (i.e., your legs will be spread with a 90-degree angle between them in the bottom position of the movement). Slowly straighten your legs to return to the starting point, and repeat the movement for the suggested number of repetitions.

Exercise Variations. When training for mass and power, keep your hips back (you should actually keep your butt in contact with the platform). To develop better frontal thigh cuts—particularly high on your thighs where the quads run into your hip girdle—you should thrust your hips forward, as in a sissy squat. Descend in normal fashion, then thrust your hips forward as you return to the erect position.

Finish

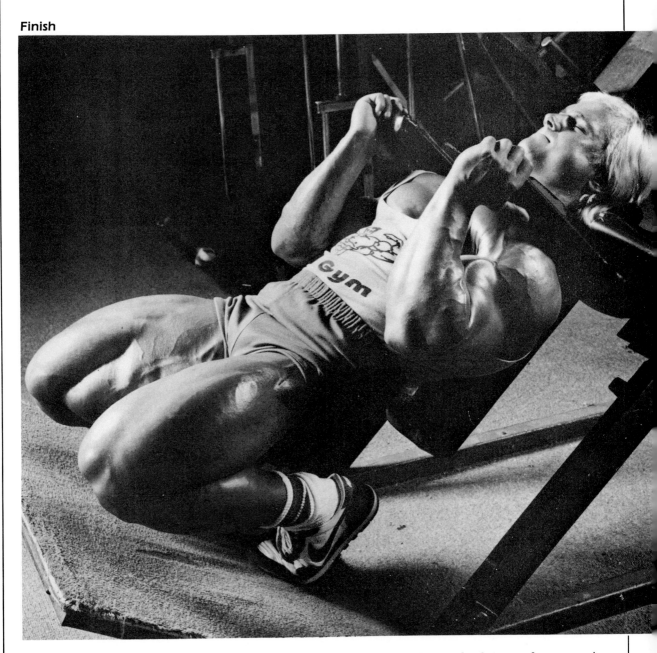

Training Tips. It's always best to push with your toes as well as your heels against the foot platform when you're doing hack squats.

Start

Standing Leg Curls

Values. This is a very direct isolation exercise for the biceps femoris (thigh biceps) at the backs of your thighs. It's also a relatively new exercise, since the machine on which it is done was invented in the early 1980s.

Starting Point. Stand facing the machine, positioning your body to the right side of the apparatus. Hook your left heel beneath the roller pad on the right side of the machine and position your left knee against the pad set at knee height directly above the roller pad. Fully straighten your left leg and help balance your weight on your right foot by grasping the uprights of the standing machine. Reverse the instructions to exercise your right leg.

Movement Performance. Slowly bend your left leg as much as possible, holding this position of the movement for a moment in order to build a peak contraction effect into the exercise. Slowly lower back to the starting point and repeat the movement for the required number of reps.

Exercise Variations. You can do this movement with your foot either pointed or flexed. Flexing your foot during leg curls isolates your calves from the exercise.

Comments. Always keep in mind that you will get a higher quality of contraction in a working muscle when you do an exercise with one limb at a time rather than two, since your mental focus need not be split between the two limbs.

Training Tips. Be sure to stretch out your hamstrings after doing leg curls, either with stiff-legged deadlifts or freehand stretching exercises.

Finish

Start/Finish

Seated Calf Raises

Values. This movement is excellent for adding width to the calves. It directly stresses the soleus, a broad, flat muscle lying beneath the gastrocnemius of your calves, which you can only exercise with your legs bent. You will also find that seated calf raises bring out the cuts on the sides of your calves.

Starting Point. Sit on the machine's seat and adjust the knee pads to an appropriate height. You can adjust these pads by removing them and then replacing a pin in the metal column attaching the pads to the lever arm of the machine. The pads should be just high enough so you can pull them over your knees when your feet are positioned on the foot crossbar. Once you have the pads over your knees, push down on your toes and then move the machine's stop bar forward to release the weight. Your toes should be about 8–10 inches (20–25 cm) apart and pointed straight ahead. Relax your calf muscles and allow your heels to sink as far below the level of your toes as possible.

Movement Performance. Use soleus and gastrocnemius strength to push down on your toes and raise your heels as high as possible above the level of your toes. Hold this top position for a moment for a peak contraction effect, lower back to the starting point, and repeat the exercise for the suggested number of reps.

Exercise Variations. If you don't have available a seated calf machine, you can still improvise this movement with a calf block, heavy barbell, and flat exercise bench. Simply pad the barbell bar with a thick towel, place it on your knees, sit at the end of the bench, and place your toes and the balls of your feet on the block of wood. You can comfortably do seated calf raises in this position.

Training Tips. There's a temptation not to stretch your heels very low in this

Midpoint

exercise, a bad mistake if you happen to make it. Much of the value of calf exercises stems from the stretch in the bottom position of the movement.

Seated Pulley Rows

Values. This is one of the best all-around back exercises in existence. It builds both thickness and width in your lats, and places significant stress on your trapezius and spinal erectors. Secondary stress is on your posterior deltoids, biceps, brachialis, and the gripping muscles of your forearms.

Starting Point. This exercise is usually performed with a handle that gives you a narrow parallel grip (with your palms facing each other). Grasp the handle, place your feet against the restraining bar near the floor pulley, and sit down on the machine's bench. Bend your legs about 10 degrees throughout the movement in order to remove harmful stress from your lower back. Fully straighten your arms and lean forward at the waist until your torso is almost touching your thighs, a position that will fully stretch your lats. For an even greater stretch in your lats, you should lower your head between your arms.

Movement Performance. Simultaneously sit erect (but avoid sitting back)

Start

Finish

and pull the handle in towards your body to touch your upper abdomen just beneath your rib cage. As you pull the handle, be sure to keep your elbows in close to your sides. And at the finish position of the movement, it's essential that you arch your back in order to completely contract your lats. Slowly return to the starting position and repeat the movement for the desired reps.

Exercise Variations. You can also do this movement with a high pulley that is set between three and four feet above the floor. And you can use a wide variety of handles attached to the end of the cable. Most frequently, you'll see bodybuilders using a handle that gives them a shoulder-width parallel grip, although you can also take a narrow-to-wide over- or undergrip on the bar.

T-Bar Rows

Values. T-bar rows develop primarily latissimus dorsi thickness. Strong secondary stress is on your spinal erectors, trapezius, posterior deltoids, biceps, brachialis, and forearm flexor muscles.

Starting Point. Place your feet on the platforms set at either side of the T-bar apparatus, with your back towards the pivot point of the bar. Reach down and grasp the handles attached to the end of the T-bar, bend your legs slightly to remove potential stress from your lower back, and hold your torso parallel with the floor. Straighten your arms fully.

Movement Performance. Without moving your torso upwards excessively, slowly pull the weight upwards until it touches your chest. Lower slowly back to the starting point and repeat the movement.

Exercise Variations. There are two types of T-bars. One is plate loaded, while the other has a cable running from

Start

Finish

the end of the bar through a pulley to a weight stack. By far, the cable-version machine gives you a longer range of motion than the plate-loaded T-bar, and it should be used whenever possible.

Training Tips. When doing T-bar rows, don't move your torso upwards and downwards during the movement, since it robs your middle back muscles of much of the desired resistance.

Start

Lat-Machine Pulldowns

Values. Lat-machine pulldowns add width to the latissimus dorsi muscles. Front pulldowns primarily stress the lower and middle sections of your lats, while pulldowns behind the neck are an upper-lat exercise. Strong secondary stress is on the posterior deltoids, biceps, brachialis, and forearm flexor muscle groups.

Starting Point. Take an overgrip on a lat-machine bar so your hands are placed about 6 inches (15 cm) wider on each side than the width of your shoulders. Fully straighten your arms and wedge your knees beneath the restraining bar below the machine to keep your body from moving as you do the exercise. Sit on the seat attached to the restraining bar. If you don't have a seat and bar, you can either sit or kneel on the floor directly beneath the pulley and have a training partner push down on your shoulders on either side of your neck to restrain your body as you do the exercise.

Movement Performance. Keeping your back arched during the exercise, slowly pull the weight downwards until it touches your upper chest in front of your neck. Slowly return to the starting position and repeat the movement.

Exercise Variations. You can also pull the lat bar down to touch your trapezius at the back of your neck. And you can use a variety of handles—one which gives you a narrow parallel grip, one with a shoulder-width parallel grip, or a straight bar handle on which you can take an undergrip. Every variation of handle or pulling angle that you employ in this exercise can help you to build more complete lats.

Finish

Hyperextensions

Values. Primary emphasis in hyperextensions is on the erector spinae muscles of your lumbar region, and secondary stress is on the hamstrings and buttocks. Unlike most lower-back exercises that place a compression stress on your lumbar vertebrae, hyperextensions are a stretching type of movement that can be comfortably and profitably performed even when you have a sore lower back.

Starting Point. Stand in a hyperextension bench facing towards the large flat pad. Lean forward and place your hips on that pad, allowing your legs to come up to the rear until the backs of your ankles rest beneath the two smaller restraining pads at the rear of the ma-

Start

Finish

chine. Keeping your legs straight, slide forward until you can comfortably hang your torso straight down from your hips. Place your hands behind your head and neck and hold them in this position throughout the movement.

Movement Performance. Using lower-back strength, slowly move your head and shoulders upwards as if performing a reverse sit-up movement. Arch your back at the top of the movement, hold this position for a moment, lower back to the starting point, and repeat the movement for the desired number of reps.

Training Tips. This movement will soon become relatively easy to perform, so once you are fully warmed up, you should add resistance to your hyperextensions by holding a light barbell plate behind your neck.

Close-Grip Chins

Values. As with other variations of chins and pulldowns, close-grip chins are primarily a lat-width building movement. Secondary stress is on the posterior deltoids, biceps, brachialis, and forearm flexor muscles. Close-grip chins stress primarily the upper sections of your lats.

Starting Point. Place a V-bar-chinning attachment over a chinning bar and grasp the handles of it with your palms towards each other. Straighten your arms fully and hang directly below the bar. You can bend your legs and cross your ankles for stability as you do this movement.

Movement Performance. Lean back throughout the exercise and slowly pull yourself up towards the bar until your upper chest touches your hands. Lower slowly back to the starting position and repeat the movement for the suggested number of repetitions.

Exercise Variations. If you don't have access to the triangle-chinning attachment, you can do close-grip chins on a chinning bar by merely switching to a narrow over- or undergrip on the bar.

Training Tips. If you're too weak to do more than about eight close-grip chins in good form, you should use a stool to help get your body up to the bar. Then from the top position you can remove your feet from the stool and work on the negative half of the movement by slowly lowering your body back to the starting point.

Start

Finish

Incline Dumbbell Presses

Values. This has become one of my key upper-body movements, and I can now do several reps with a pair of 180-pound dumbbells. Incline dumbbell presses place primary stress on the upper pectorals, anterior deltoids, and triceps.

Start

They are particularly good for developing excellent pec-delt tie-ins. Strong secondary stress is on the lower and outer pecs, medial deltoids, and the upper-back muscles that impart rotational force on your scapulae.

Starting Point. A lot of the trick in this exercise lies in getting the dumbbells up to the starting point of the movement. Grasp two moderately heavy weights in your hands and rest the dumbbells on end on your knees. Pull your left knee upwards to bring the dumbbell in your left hand up to your shoulder, then immediately repeat the process with your right knee. Then you can press the weights above your head with your palms facing forward. Alternatively, you can have two strong training partners hand you the weights at your shoulders, although you'll find it a little difficult to have them release the weights precisely together.

Movement Performance. Keep your elbows back and slowly lower the dumbbells downwards until they touch your shoulders. If at all possible, actually lower the weights *below* the level of your shoulders. Press the dumbbells back to straight arm's length directly above your shoulder joints and repeat the movement for the suggested number of reps.

Exercise Variations. A few bodybuilders do dumbbell incline presses with their palms facing inward rather than straight forward. You should also vary the angle of incline bench on which you do the movement. Normally, bodybuilders use a 45-degree incline bench, but a 30-degree bench (or one even a little lower) tends to stress the pecs more intensely.

Finish

Pec-Deck Flyes

Values. This movement has only evolved in recent years, but most larger bodybuilding gyms now have a pec-deck apparatus. Pec-deck flyes stress the entire pectoral muscle mass quite intensely, particularly the inner pecs where they originate along your sternum (breastbone).

Starting Point. Adjust the height of the machine's seat so your upper arms are parallel to the floor when you sit on the seat and do the movement. The bench can be adjusted either by repositioning a pin that holds it, or by spinning the seat upwards or downwards. Sit on the seat and force one elbow and forearm behind the pad, resting your fingers lightly over the top of the movement pad. Rotate your body to the other side and place your elbow and forearm against that pad in the same way. Sit facing directly forward and allow the weight on the machine to pull your elbows as far to the rear as possible.

Movement Performance. Use pectoral strength to move your elbows and the pads forward and inward towards each other until they touch directly in front of your chest. Hold this peak contracted position for a moment, return to the starting point, and repeat the movement for the required number of repetitions.

Exercise Variations. For a slightly different stress on your pectorals, move the seat slightly upwards or downwards from the basic position. It's also possible to do this movement one arm at a time.

Near Start

Finish

Cable Crossovers

Values. Crossovers are primarily performed during a precontest cycle to carve deep striations across the pecs. Primarily, cable crossovers stress the lower, outer, and inner sections of the pectorals.

Starting Point. Attach loop handles to two high pulleys, grasp the handles in your hands, and stand directly between the two pulleys with your feet set about shoulder-width apart. Lean slightly forward at the waist and keep that torso angle throughout the movement. Rotate your hands so your palms are facing towards the floor and extend your arms upwards from your shoulders at approximately 45-degree angles on either side.

Movement Performance. Use pectoral strength to move your hands slowly downwards and towards each other in semicircular arcs until they touch 4–6 inches (10–15 cm) in front of your hips. Hold your hands in this position for a few seconds, tensing your pecs and delts as if performing a "most muscular" pose. Return your hands slowly back along the same arcs to the starting point and repeat the exercise.

Exercise Variations. You can also do this exercise while kneeling on the floor between the two pulleys—which isolates your legs from the movement—as well as with one arm at a time.

Start

Finish

Seated Dumbbell Presses

Start

Values. Dumbbell presses directly stress the anterior heads of your deltoids and your triceps. Secondary stress is on your medial and posterior delts, upper-chest, and upper-back muscles.

Starting Point. Grasp two moderately heavy dumbbells and sit down at the end of a flat exercise bench. If possible, sit on a bench that has an upright support against which you can rest your back during the movement. Hook your feet around the upright legs of the bench to restrain your body in position as you do the movement. Clean the dumbbells up to your shoulders, then rotate your wrists so your palms are facing towards your body.

Movement Performance. Slowly press the dumbbells directly upwards, simultaneously rotating your hands so your palms are facing away from your body at the conclusion of the movement when the dumbbells are held with elbows locked directly above your shoulder joints and head. Slowly lower the dumbbells back to the starting point, rotating your hands back to the position in which they are facing towards your body. Repeat the exercise for the desired number of repetitions.

Exercise Variation. You can also do this dumbbell press in a standing position.

Training Tips. The farther down your chest you lower the dumbbells, the greater the stretch in your deltoid muscles at the start of the movement and the more you ultimately get out of doing the exercise.

Midpoint

Finish

Upright Rows

Values. Upright rows stress all of the muscles of the shoulder girdle and are one of the best upper-body movements.

Upright rows place very direct stress on the anterior and medial deltoids, trapezius, biceps, brachialis, and forearm flexor muscles.

Start

Finish

Starting Point. Take a narrow undergrip in the middle of a moderately heavy barbell, about 6 inches (15 cm) between your index fingers. Place your feet about shoulder-width apart and stand erect with your arms held straight down at your sides and the barbell in your hands resting across your upper thighs.

Movement Performance. Without moving your torso, slowly bend your arms and pull the barbell up the front of your body (it should travel no more than a few inches forward of your body) until your hands touch the bottom of your chin. Be sure as you pull the barbell upwards that your elbows are always held above the level of your hands, particularly in the top position of the movement. As soon as your hands touch your chin, roll your shoulders backwards and squeeze your shoulder blades together. Slowly lower the weight back to the starting point and repeat the movement for the required number of reps.

Exercise Variations. You can also do upright rows with a bar handle attached to the cable running through a floor pulley, or even while holding two moderately heavy dumbbells in your hands. Do whichever feels best for you.

Bent Laterals

Values. This fine isolation movement places very direct stress on the posterior heads of your deltoids and secondary stress on your trapezius and other upper-back muscles.

Starting Point. Grasp two light dumbbells in your hands and set your feet about shoulder-width apart. Unlock

Start

Finish

your legs throughout the movement to remove potential stress from your lower back. Bend over until your torso is parallel to the floor and hang your arms directly down from your shoulders. Rotate your hands so your palms are facing towards each other and slightly bend your arms during the exercise.

Movement Performance. Without altering the position of your legs or torso, slowly raise the dumbbells directly out to the sides and upwards until they are slightly above the level of your shoulders. Slowly lower them back along the same arcs to the starting point and repeat the movement for the suggested number of reps.

Exercise Variations. This movement is frequently performed while sitting on the end of a flat exercise bench and bending forward until your torso is resting on your thighs as you do the exercise. Or you can do your bent laterals with either two cables (they will cross each other beneath your body) at once, or a single cable handle held in one hand (the cable will pass diagonally beneath your torso).

Barbell Preacher Curls

Near Start

Values. Barbell preacher curls stress the entire biceps muscle group, but particularly the lower section of the biceps muscle where it inserts into the forearm. Secondary stress is on the powerful forearm flexors.

Starting Point. Take an undergrip on a barbell with your hands set 2–3 inches (5–8 cm) wider on each side than the width of your shoulders. Lean over the top of a preacher bench with the top edge wedged beneath your armpits. Run your upper arms straight down the angled surface of the bench parallel to each other, then fully straighten your arms.

Movement Performance. Use your biceps strength to slowly curl the barbell in a semicircular arc from the starting point up to a position directly under your chin. Flex your biceps as hard as you can in this position, then slowly lower the weight back to the starting position. Repeat.

Exercise Variations. You can do reverse preacher curls with a barbell to stress your brachialis and forearm supinator muscles more strongly. You can also do preacher curls with a straight bar attached to a floor pulley, with two dumbbells, or with a single dumbbell held in one hand. You can even do narrow-grip preacher curls with an E-Z curl bar.

Training Tips. Be very careful to avoid bouncing the bar in the bottom position of the movement, since it places your lower biceps in a poor mechanical position and can injure them.

Midpoint

Close-Grip Bench Presses

Values. This is an excellent movement for many of your upper-body muscles, particularly for your triceps, inner pectorals, and anterior deltoids.

Starting Point. Place a barbell on the support rack of a pressing bench and load it up with a moderate poundage. Lie back on the bench with your shoulders about 4 inches (10 cm) from the support uprights and balance your body in position by placing your feet flat on the floor. Take a narrow overgrip in the middle of the bar, about 6 inches (15 cm) of space showing between your index fingers. Straighten your arms and bring the bar-

Start/Finish

Midpoint

bell forward to a position supported by straight arms directly above your chest and shoulders.

Movement Performance. Keeping your elbows in close to your torso during the movement, slowly bend your arms and lower the barbell down to lightly touch the middle your chest. Without bouncing the bar off your chest, slowly push it back to starting position. Repeat the movement for the suggested number of reps.

Exercise Variations. You can vary the grip from one as narrow as having your hands touching each other in the middle of the bar to one as wide as the bar allows. You can also do close-grip benches on low-incline or low-decline benches.

Parallel Bar Dips

Values. When performed with your torso held bolt upright, parallel bar dips place a great deal of stress on your triceps muscles, as well as on your anterior deltoids and lower pectorals.

Starting Point. Jump up on the parallel bars with your palms facing inward towards each other and your torso supported with elbows locked above the bars. Keep your legs relatively straight and your torso totally upright as you do the exercise.

Movement Performance. Keeping your elbows in tight against your torso, slowly bend your arms and lower your body as far below the level of the parallel bars as possible. Push yourself back up to the starting point and repeat the movement for an appropriate number of reps.

Training Tips. As soon as you can comfortably perform at least 12 reps in this movement, you should add resistance to it by strapping a light dumbbell around your waist with a rope or loop of nylon webbing.

Midpoint

One-Arm Dumbbell Wrist Curls

Values. One-arm dumbbell wrist curls are always performed with your palm facing upwards to directly stress the powerful flexor muscles on the inner sides of your forearms.

Starting Point. Grasp a moderately heavy dumbbell in your left hand and sit

Start

Finish

down straddling a flat exercise bench in such a position that you can run your left forearm down the bench, hanging your wrist and hand off the end of the bench, your palm facing upwards.

Movement Performance. Flex your wrist and curl the dumbbell upwards in a small semicircular arc to as high a position as possible. Return slowly to the starting point and repeat the move-ment for the required number of repetitions.

Training Tips. To achieve a peak contraction in your forearm flexor muscles, you should elevate the end of the bench away from your working hand by placing a thick block of wood under the bench legs. Alternatively, you can do this exercise on a preacher bench that has been set at a 30-degree angle.

Sit-Ups

Values. Sit-ups stress the entire rectus abdominis muscle wall, particularly the upper half of the frontal abs. And if you do the movement in a twisting manner, you can also stress your intercostal muscles.

Starting Point. Lie on your back on an abdominal board with your feet towards the top end. Hook your toes beneath the roller pads or strap provided at that end to restrain your body during the movement. Keep your legs bent about 15 degrees throughout the movement in order to remove potentially harmful stress from your lower back. Place your hands behind your head and neck and hold them in that position throughout your set.

Movement Performance. Slowly curl your torso off the abdominal board by first lifting your head and shoulders, then your upper back, middle back, and lower back, until your torso is at a 90-degree angle with your thighs. Slowly lower yourself back to the starting point by reversing the procedure. Repeat the movement for an appropriate number of reps.

Exercise Variations. By twisting to each side on succeeding reps, you can involve both your rectus abdominis and intercostals. On both twisting and normal sit-ups, you can make the movement more intense by either raising the foot end of the board, or by holding a light dumbbell behind your neck as you do the exercise.

Start

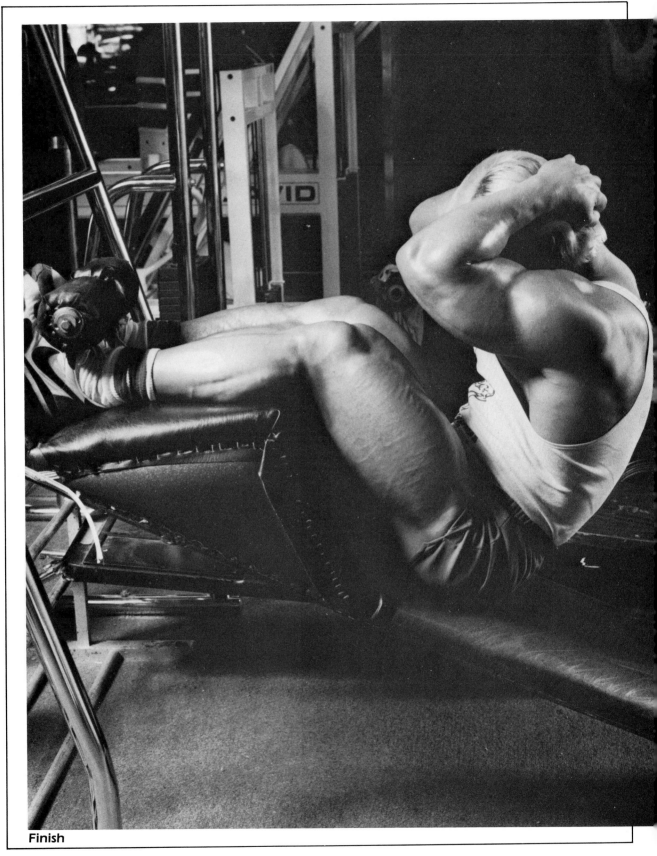

Finish

Crunches

Values. This is one of the best rectus abdominis exercises. When correctly performed, it stresses the entire frontal abdominal wall. And you can even stress your intercostals if you do the movement with a slight twist to each side.

Starting Point. Lie on your back on the gym floor or a mat in a position where you can rest your lower legs over a flat exercise bench. When your legs are in the correct position, your thighs will be at a right angle with your torso and your lower legs will be at a right angle to your thighs. Place your hands either behind your head and neck or rest them over your chest.

Movement Performance. You must simultaneously perform four functions to

Start

Finish

correctly do the crunch movement: (1) Use lower abdominal strength to lift your hips from the floor (be careful, however, that you don't lift your hips by pulling with your hamstrings); (2) Use upper abdominal strength to lift your head and shoulders from the floor; (3) Attempt to force your shoulders towards your hips, essentially shortening your torso; and (4) Forcefully exhale. When you correctly and simultaneously perform all four functions, you will feel a powerful contraction in your abdominals. Hold this contraction for a moment, lower back to the starting point, and continue the movement until your abdominals are fully fatigued.

Exercise Variations. After you have performed several reps straight forward, try alternately twisting to each side with succeeding reps.

Seated Twists/Side Bends

Values. This combination of two exercises directly stresses the external, internal, and transverse obliques.

Starting Point. Sit on a flat exercise bench and either place your feet flat on the floor or intertwine them in the up-

Start

right legs of the bench to keep your hips from moving during the exercise. Place a broomstick across your shoulders and behind your neck, wrapping your arms around it to secure the broomstick in position.

Movement Performance. Twist rhythmically from one side to the other, being sure to get a very hard contraction in your obliques at the end of each repetition. And after you have done at least 25 reps in each direction, do side bends, bending as far to one side as you comfortably can, then back to the other side.

Finish

Training Tips. The key to correctly performing this movement is to keep your hips immobile. You'll often see uninformed bodybuilders doing these movements in a standing position, moving their hips along with their torsos and getting zilch from the movement. Don't make the same mistake.

Level-Three Workout

This training program may cause a little confusion, because it can be used for either off-season or precontest routines. For an experienced bodybuilder—one with at least two or three years of steady training—it would be appropriate for off-season use. But for less experienced bodybuilders, it is best used as a precontest routine.

At this level, I recommend using a four-day training cycle, three training days followed by a day of total rest from the weights (although not necessarily from aerobic training). This will involve training a lot of weekends, but that's one price you will have to pay in order to become a champion bodybuilder.

I caution you not to get too locked into this four-day cycle, particularly in the off-season. Listen to your body; if it tells you that it's too depleted of energy, take an extra rest day. This can either be interspersed between any of the three training days, or added to the normal rest interval between them.

It's very important as you grow more experienced in bodybuilding that you allow your body to fully recuperate between workouts. Without complete recuperation, you definitely won't experience optimum muscle growth. If you are not recuperating sufficiently between workouts, you should either shorten your training sessions or take more rest days between workouts.

DAY ONE   (Chest, Back, Abs)

	Sets	Reps
Incline Dumbbell Presses (warm up, then work up to . . .)	3–4	5*
Additional Incline Dumbbell Presses	1	10†
Dumbbell Flyes (flat bench)	3	8–12*
Parallel Bar Dips	1–2	10–15†
Close-grip Chins	3	max
Seated Pulley Rows	3	8–10*
Cross-bench Pullovers	2	15
Roman Chair Sit-ups	3–4	25–30
Crunches	3–4	20–25
Seated Twists/Side Bends	3–4	50

DAY TWO
(Thighs, Lower Back, Calves)

	Sets	Reps
Squats (warm up, then work up to . . .)	4–5	8–10
Hack Squats (sissy-squat style)	3	8–10*
Leg Extensions	3	8–10*
Lying Leg Curls	3	8–10*
Standing Leg Curls	2–3	8–10*
Hyperextensions (every second or third workout, do deadlifts for five or six reps per set)	3–4	10–15
Seated Calf Raises	4–6	6–20**
Standing Calf Raises	2–3	10–12*

DAY THREE
(Shoulders, Arms, Abs)

	Sets	Reps
Seated Dumbbell Presses	4	8–10*
Upright Rows	3–4	8–10*
Bent Laterals	3–4	8–10*
Barbell Preacher Curls	4	8–10**
Seated Dumbbell Curls	4	8–10*
Close-grip Bench Presses	4–5	8–10*
Parallel Bar Dips	4–5	8–10**
One-arm Wrist Curls	4–5	10–12**
Bench Leg Raises	3–4	25–30
Incline Sit-ups	3–4	20–25

*Continue each of these sets to failure.

**Continue the final two or three sets to failure.

†With a moderate weight only, as a warm-down set.

Level-Four Workout

Bodybuilders gain an advantage metabolically by training more and more frequently as a competition approaches. Frequent workouts—whether they be with weights or some type of aerobics session—stimulate your Basal Metabolic Rate (BMR) and help you to burn off fat more quickly. Therefore, a four-day training cycle may not be appropriate for some bodybuilders, particularly not for those who experience difficulty in getting cut up for a competition.

The best alternative to the four-day cycle during a peaking phase is six-day-per-week training. There are two types of six-day split routines: 1) each major muscle group is worked twice per week (abs, chest, shoulders, and triceps on Monday and Thursday—calves, upper back, biceps, and forearms on Tuesday and Friday—abs, thighs, lower back, and neck on Wednesday and Saturday); 2) a more intense split in which each major group is stressed three times per week (abs, chest, back, and shoulders on Monday-Wednesday-Friday—calves, thighs, and arms on Tuesday-Thursday-Saturday).

You should now know which exercises affect specific body parts, so you can easily make up your own precontest six-day split routines by choosing the exercises from the preceding Level-Three Workout and scheduling them on the appropriate workout days.

Tom Platz's Precontest Program

My off-season routine at the end of Chapter 4 is the same as my precontest training program. The only differences prior to a competition are as follows:

1. The natural enthusiasm generated by an upcoming major competition tends to make me push significantly harder than during an off-season training cycle. I tend to use my heaviest weights of the year a week prior to a competition—despite having low energy levels due to dieting—because of this newfound drive.

2. I might occasionally do two or three more total sets per muscle group, depending on how completely my body is recuperating between workouts.

3. I might also skip a normally schedule rest day if I am recuperating well.

4. I double, triple, and then quadruple the amount of aerobic training I perform. Depending on how close the competition is and how far I still must go to be totally peaked out, I may do as many as two or three hours of aerobics each day.

5. I attain the deepest possible tan (see Chapter 9).

6. I spend up to two hours per day practicing my posing. Not only does this make my routine more effective, but it also helps to harden up my physique by burning off additional calories and improving the control I have over my flexed muscles.

7. I know I've already emphasized how important I feel the mental aspect of bodybuilding is, but I *do* max out my mental approach to the sport as I am peaking for a Mr. Olympia contest. It's important enough to master the mental side of bodybuilding for you to read Chapter 8 a number of times.

There you have it—Tom Platz-style, no-frills peaking! Give it a try!

8 Winning Mental Approach

If you can learn to harness the full potential of your mind, it can become a powerful force in shaping your physique, as well as every other aspect of your life. The human mind has created the baffling array of space-age technology that we see about us every day; certainly you can use your own mind to build the ultimate, award-winning physique.

You need only to follow a few simple steps to fully master your mental powers. You must initially program your mind to aid yourself in reaching your bodybuilding goals. Then you must constantly update your mind-computer program to keep improving as a bodybuilder.

Positive Thinking

The essence of any successful athlete's mental attitude is positive thinking. You must be positive above all else, even when a negative experience arises. If you've never had a negative experience in any respect, how could you possibly establish a reference point to determine what a positive experience will be? Therefore, in this way you can profit greatly from an occasional negative experience. Just make up your mind not to live in a predominantly negative realm.

I believe in living a rich, full, enjoyable life, so I choose to live positively. If you expect success, you will get success; but if you expect failure, you inevitably get failure. You are in total control of your destiny. No one is responsible for your success or failure but you. And you can't blame anyone or anything for a failure. Everyone feels negative at times. I certainly have. Learn from these negative experiences and apply them later to positive approaches to life and bodybuilding. One thing you should always remember is that everything—regardless of how dark it might seem at the time—always works out for the best.

Unless my mind triggers the will to improve my physique, it won't happen. Essentially, the mind is the master potentiator in bodybuilding. I've actually trained optimally and dieted very strictly for more than two months before a competition, but ended up failing miserably to reach peak contest condition simply because my mind wasn't into the peaking process. I may have eaten less than 1200 calories a day of chicken breasts, fish, and salad, but I actually looked as if I'd been on a diet of jelly doughnuts without the correct mental approach.

When I permit something to happen mentally, it soon happens physically as well. Just as I can't get ripped up in my contest cycle unless I think about getting ripped, I also can't gain muscle mass unless I mentally permit it to happen.

At the 1980 Mr. Olympia contest, I competed at a bodyweight of 208 pounds. For 1981, I mentally programmed myself to weigh 220, just as cut but with even greater muscle mass and physical proportions than the year before. As soon as I returned to Santa Monica following the 1980 Mr. Olympia, I began to think about becoming a massive 230 pounds and then training down to a diamond-hard 220 for the next Mr. Olympia.

Once I was thinking this way, I began to pack on muscle mass very quickly, until in the middle of July 1981, I could look in the mirror and see precisely the degree of muscle mass and density that I had visualized for myself at the point where I would begin my precontest training and dietary cycle. Coincidentally, although I had not weighed myself in nine months, I stepped on the scales and weighed 230½ pounds, only a half pound off my goal! This remarkable fact further validates the power of a bodybuilder's mind.

I immediately programmed myself to slowly train down to a ripped-to-shreds 220 pounds for the Mr. Olympia contest in October. And because I permitted this to happen mentally, it absolutely did happen physically, and I reached my lifetime best condition to place third in the contest. If you expect success—and you expect it beyond a shadow of a doubt—you *will* succeed.

Every negative situation can and must be made positive. If you hate to see a particular photo of yourself, for example, analyze it to discover what makes you look so bad. Then change either your physique or the pose to your satisfaction. Always program your mind to learn from your mistakes.

On the other side of the coin, when you doubt yourself and expect failure, you will very definitely fail. Hundreds of bodybuilders—and thousands of other athletes—actually fail because they fear success in their sport. To them, there are overwhelming responsibilities that go with success (e.g., having to maintain a high level of physical condition after winning a contest because friends and family members expect you to win again and again, ad infinitum). This fear of success guarantees failure.

You have nothing to fear if you become a winning bodybuilder, because at the higher levels of the sport you actually compete only against yourself. Indeed, there are many attractive possibilities that come with being a winner. For example, I have been able to make a handsome living solely from professional bodybuilding ever since I won the IFBB Mr. Universe title in 1978. And more intrinsically, the self-satisfaction I receive each year from constantly improving is more than enough to maintain my enthusiasm for the sport.

I take an extremely positive approach not only to bodybuilding, but also to every other facet of my life. As a successful bodybuilder, I am fascinated with applying my winning mental attitude and abundant energies to other parts of my life. Following Arnold Schwarzenegger's lead, I am an athlete in the morning and a businessman in the afternoon. And business is great!

My father, a vice-president for Equitable Life insurance company, gives motivational speeches to the executives of his company each week. He's so impressed with my positive approach to bodybuilding and life in general that he now frequently has me speak, too. Even though these men and women aren't athletes, they're very receptive to my message, undoubtedly because the mental rules for success in bodybuilding are the same as in any other walk of life.

Arnold Schwarzenegger is a perfect example of a positive approach to life. When Arnold came over from Europe in 1968 to train in California, he could speak only a few words of English. But he knew America was the land of opportunity for an intelligent and enterprising individual. He expected success and never allowed doubt or fear to enter his mind. He's now a millionaire many times over, the world's greatest bodybuilder, and an international film star.

To me, learning that you have the ability to become a superman simply by eliminating fear and doubt and replacing them with positive mental attitudes is of utmost importance. That's why in my bodybuilding seminars I try as hard as I can to help my students find this intangible mental ability within themselves and realize that with it they can do literally anything.

Visualization

Visualization is the technique by which you can positively program your mind to help you reach your bodybuilding goals. It involves a practical application of what psychologists call *self-actualization*. Through visualization you can conciously program your subconscious mind in any manner you desire.

For example, think about someone you've known who had wanted to become a doctor, lawyer, piano virtuoso, whatever. Those who have successfully reached their goals are the ones whose desire to succeed was so strong that they actually lived the occupation of their choice of daydreams. The subconscious mind can be programmed to pave the route to the desired goal. With strong desire it becomes easy, for example, to sit down for six hours and practice a Brahms concerto time after time.

In normal self-actualization one needn't do anything more than creatively daydream about become a certain type of person or holding a particular job. In visualization we consciously and realistically seek to program our subconscious mind to help us make bodybuilding decisions an easy task. When this is properly done, it's no longer an ordeal to diet or train. The entire bodybuilding process becomes a joyful experience. I can assure you of this, because my bodybuilding preparations are the best part of my life.

To properly visualize your bodybuilding success, you should be relaxed and free from distractions for at least 15–20 minutes. When starting, I think you can best practice visualization while lying in bed preparing to sleep. Then you should be relaxed and have a minimum potential for disruption of your thought processes. It's a good idea to practice visualization in the dark, at bedtime.

As you lie in bed, imagine yourself as you would like to become one day. Gradually make this image more and more sharp, until it is almost as if you are projecting a film against the inside of your eyelids. Vividly visualize every lump of muscle, every cut between muscle groups, and every vein on your body. Imagine in detail what it would feel like to be inside that new body, to walk onstage at a major competition and hear the audience shout its approval of your efforts.

Every workout begins in the mind! (*Craig Dietz*)

Actually, this feeling of what it would be like inside a great physique is crucial to optimum visualization practice and results. Normally you would visualize yourself with only one of your five senses, the imagined sense of vision. And this is as far as virtually all bodybuilders and other athletes take visualization. But psychologists have determined that you can get a great deal more out of visualization practice if you also involve some of your other four senses—touch, hearing, taste, and smell—in your visualized image. They talk about a "three out of five" rule, in which an athlete endeavors to involve three of his or her five senses in the visualization practice.

In my own experience, visualization is more than twice as effective if you can visualize with at least three of your five senses. And if you can involve all five senses—a relatively easy process once you know how to do it—I'm confident that you will triple the results of your visualization practice. As bodybuilders, we should consistently involve five senses in our visualized images.

Let's walk through an example of how you can involve sight, touch, hearing, taste, and smell in a single visualized image. Lie back in a comfortable position and fully relax your mind and body. Then begin to conjure up the image of your fantastic new physique. That involves the sense of sight, or at least the imagined sense of sight.

Next imagine yourself inside that body, sensing your muscles straining to burst through your superthin skin. This is the imagined sense of touch. Savor it by walking about the room in your imagination, feeling your leg muscles powerfully contract and relax with each step. I do this quite often myself. In my visualized image, I can feel myself walking onstage for a competition, and I can even look down at my feet and see them leading me towards the posing platform.

The sense of hearing is relatively easy to add to your visualized image. I continue to imagine walking onstage for my Mr. Olympia competition by hearing the huge roar that comes up from the audience when they first see me step from behind the curtains, as well as when I am powerfully and gracefully going through my posing routine. Alternatively, you can visualize yourself during a heavy workout, feel your muscles straining against the weights, and hear the deep-throated rattle of several 45-pound plates on the ends of the Olympic bar you're using.

You can involve your sense of smell in a number of ways. Imagine the scent of the oil you've rubbed into your skin to highlight your body's amazing muscularity. You could simply add all of this into your image of the new you posing at a major competition. Other common olfactory experiences include the smell of honest sweat on your body as you blast away during a workout, and the aroma of the food you're eating while on a precontest diet.

Your fifth sense, that of taste, most easily comes into play in imagining yourself eating one of your final precontest meals. That dry piece of fish or skinned chicken breast may not taste like much, but you can visualize how great your physique appears as you're eating it. You can believe this—it'll feel absolutely great! This type of five-sense visualization will dramatically assist you in attaining your desired image.

Regularity is a key in visualization practice. After a few months your subconscious mind will be strongly programmed for success. Ultimately, visualization should become as much of an ingrained habit as brushing your teeth or combing your hair. And you must constantly update your visualized image of your physique, or you won't continue to improve.

I visualize two things each day: how I will look at the next Mr. Olympia contest and how my entire superproductive workout will go that day. But I'm always realistic about my visualizations. You have to be realistic and objective as you visualize yourself. If you are four feet tall, you aren't going to play professional basketball, are you? Take into consideration the strengths and weaknesses of your physique, as well as what you can realistically expect at contest time from your optimum training and dietary preparations. Set your target high, but not so high that you can't hit it.

Each morning before I go to the gym, I picture every set and every rep of my workout, feeling the superpump I'll get from it. I do this every day, either just before breakfast or while drinking my cup of coffee. I used to also visualize my poundages for each set, but I don't anymore. Now my emphasis is more on how the working muscle *feels* than on the actual weight being used.

While I recommend that you practice visualization before falling asleep, I've become so adept at this practice that I can do it throughout the day. When my posing music ("Ride Like the Wind" by Christopher Cross) comes on the radio, for example, it invariably sets me to visualizing.

There are a lot of other tricks I use to put myself in the correct frame of mind to win a competition. Before my Mr. Universe win, for example, I had a sign that said, TOM PLATZ—MR. UNIVERSE hung over my posing mirror so I'd see it constantly. In my training and nutrition log I'd sometimes write out an autograph, "Tom Platz—Mr. Universe," just to get used to seeing it and foster the belief that I was already Mr. Universe. Now I write "Tom Platz—Mr. Olympia" in my diary, although I have yet to actually win it.

Concentration

In my training seminars I always talk about concentration, or the strong link I have forged between my mind and my working muscles as I am training. I believe that my ability to concentrate fully on a given muscle group is better now than it's ever been, and my results are coming more quickly than ever before as a result. I can walk into the gym in any mood, sort of snap my fingers, and presto! I'm right into working a particular muscle optimally.

In past years I'd attribute a good workout to something I'd eaten the night before, but never to my mental state. Once I became conscious of my mental attitude, however, it was apparent that eating a piece of dry whole-grain toast wasn't the crucial factor. It was mental attitude and concentration that gave me optimum workouts. And once I realized this, I could get in a great workout almost every time I trained.

To develop good concentration, constantly experiment, trying different exercises and workouts. Consciously imagine your working muscles extending and contracting under a heavy load. And if you don't know which muscles are being worked by a particular movement, read enough anatomy and kinesiology books to find out. Look up the muscles on an anatomy chart so you know which ones you should be feeling as you do an exercise. You'd be amazed at how many young bodybuilders do an exercise with no clear idea of what muscle it's supposed to build up.

Everyone can sense when he's had a good workout. Sometimes it just happens, but you're unsure of why. Analyze everything in your training diary—including your state of mind—after you've had a good workout. Then try to duplicate the conditions and see if you have another good one. When you are able to concentrate totally on a working muscle group for an entire set—projecting your mental focus so intensely that you actually seem to *become* the muscle that you're working—shoot for additional sets of equal intensity.

You can't expect to be able to fully concentrate after your first workout, nor after your hundredth. It takes at least two or three years before you have the type of concentration that allows you to shut out the world during a set. When you can do a set of concentration curls and not notice that a truck has crashed into the side of the gym, you have developed a proper level of workout concentration.

Goal Setting

Every young bodybuilder wants to make it to the top as quickly as possible. And in his zeal to achieve a championship physique, he is often overwhelmed by the task at hand. He takes one look at his puny physique and another at the photos of superstar bodybuilders in various muscle magazines, and his task seems impossibly difficult. If he takes things one small step at a time, however, he will have less problems with achieving his goal of possessing a herculean physique.

Every complex idea—or major goal—can be simplified, depending on how you approach it. A complex idea is really just a group of simple ones. When you're faced with a mind-boggling goal, you should simply break it down into smaller, more manageable goals. And each little goal that is achieved brings you one step closer to your ultimate goal.

Let's say that you're now doing six reps of bench presses with 250 pounds and you understand that your pecs, delts, and triceps will be more massive and muscular if you can do this same six reps with 300 pounds. However, it's tough for the average bodybuilder to accept the idea of handling 50 pounds

more in a bench press set. An additional five pounds each month doesn't sound that bad, however, and ten increments of five pounds each inevitably add up to 50 pounds over ten months.

As soon as you reach a goal, you must immediately set another one. And believe me, you'll reach these goals and soon be able to win big competitions.

The Psychological Edge

You must consistently see yourself as a winner to establish a positive self-image. I feel that you have to be truly willing to give your all as a bodybuilder in order to open the path to success. But you must be able to rationalize it if you don't get everything you've set as your goal in the sport, and still see yourself as a winner for achieving what you have.

You must also realize that there's a risk involved—such as the risk of failure—in any success venture, and especially in bodybuilding. Still, I always expect my training to work, because you have to expect and create success. Too much of anything—training, social life, or whatever—is counterproductive. And even though a risk is involved in your bodybuilding, it isn't a suicide mission. It's a calculated risk that you have to take in an effort to win. You might lose, but hopefully you will win every competition you enter.

Self-Confidence

There's no question that a healthy degree of cockiness adds to a pro bodybuilder's appeal. Unquestionably, Arnold Schwarzenegger was physically the greatest bodybuilder of all time, but he was made even greater in the eyes of his fans by the charming degree of cockiness that he displayed onstage in his duels with Lou Ferrigno, Frank Zane, and Franco Columbu. Muhammad Ali was to boxing what Arnold was to bodybuilding. Ali was a technically great boxer, but he'd be far less memorable if he hadn't been so self-assured in and out of the ring.

While a degree of cockiness is something you should strive for in your onstage personality, be very careful that you don't move from cocky to arrogant in your attitude towards your friends and fans. As you become a champion bodybuilder and are looked up to by hundreds and thousands of younger athletes, it's best to be both friendly and humble in your dealings with the public. This way you'll make a far better statement for yourself and for the sport of bodybuilding in general.

I am always deadly serious in my bodybuilding endeavors, but sometimes I have to stand back and laugh at myself. Bodybuilding is fraught with frustration, and sometimes you really can't do a thing but laugh about a mistake you've made. Then get back into the gym with an improved self-confidence and pump some really heavy iron!

Stop to Smell the Flowers

One of the worst things you can do is to devote yourself totally to bodybuilding. I've seen hundreds of young men make this mistake over the years, and they pay dearly for it. Not only will they have nothing to fall back on if they don't make it to the top and earn big bucks as pro bodybuilders, but their total dedication to the sport can actually hold back their progress.

The best bodybuilders whom I have known over the years have a great diversity of interests. Certainly, they are 100 percent dedicated to their sport when they're in the gym, but that is only two or three hours per day. The rest of the day true pro champions occupy themselves with business matters, furthering their educations, their family lives, and other hobbies.

Living, eating, and sleeping bodybuilding 24 hours per day will ultimately burn you out, and you'll fail to make big gains. My best advice to you is to keep bodybuilding in its proper perspective, as a valuable adjunct to the rest of your life.

Above all else, don't sacrifice your education to the gods of bodybuilding. Even if you have to cut a workout short here and there to have time for your studies, you'll come out ahead in the long run. I didn't move from Michigan to California to devote myself to my sport until I had earned two college degrees and had job skills that I could rely on while I was working myself up the ladder. And if I hadn't made it as a successful professional bodybuilder, I'd have been able to fall back on these skills and have a good full-time job to support my bodybuilding hobby.

Don't sacrifice your social life or family life in blind pursuit of a goal. It's simply not worth it, because one day you will no longer be a competitive bodybuilder and the sport will take a less important place in your life. Then you will need to have a wealth of friends and relatives to give you the emotional support that everyone needs.

My own life is very full. I am a bodybuilder only in the morning when I am training; the rest of the day I am a human being. I work on my business, I work on my social life, and I work at furthering my education. In short, I stop to smell the flowers, and I'm far better off for it. If I hadn't done this, I would be a less complete person, and I am very sure that I would never have reached my current level of physical and mental development.

9 Bodybuilding Competition

The ultimate object for many bodybuilders is to enter competitions and soon start taking home first-place trophies by the carload. Assuming that you've been following all of my advice up to this point and have begun to approach your lifetime best condition, it's time that you learn a little more about the actual process of a major bodybuilding show and how you should prepare for it.

In this chapter, I'll teach you how to pose for all three rounds of posing under the IFBB system of judging, plus explain the finer points of a competition posedown. I'll also discuss contest grooming and tanning, what to expect once you're at a competition, and finally give you a definition of a winning bodybuilder.

Bodybuilding Posing

In order to assess a bodybuilder's all-around physical development, the IFBB has evolved a judging system that consists of three distinctly different rounds of posing, each of which is individually evaluated. And at the end of a competition, a posedown is conducted among the top five contestants following the initial three rounds of posing. This IFBB judging system is universally followed by the NPC, AFWB, CAFB, and more than 115 other national bodybuilding federations.

Round-One Poses

In Round One of the IFBB judging system, you will be required to perform seven compulsory poses: front double biceps, front lat spread, side chest (from either side), back double biceps, back lat spread, side triceps (again, from either side), and a front abdominal pose with one leg extended forward to display thigh and calf development. This round of standard compulsory poses reveals your general development under equal conditions with the rest of your competitors.

I feel that it's essential that you have an outstanding front double biceps pose in your repertoire because it is the first pose that the judges will see you perform. Communications researchers—most notably Marshall McLuhan—have concluded that first impressions are vital; if someone is impressed with you from the start, it will be more likely that he or she will remain impressed by you. Therefore, you *must* get your front double biceps shot down cold.

There are two primary ways in which you can use your torso muscles in a double biceps shot. You can either do the pose with a stomach vacuum, or with your abdominals crunched down. With a vacuum, you will have more sweep to your lats and will present an image of slightly greater overall upper-body mass. You lose this V-tapered look to your torso when you crunch down on your abs, but you also gain greater impressiveness through your midsection. It's really a toss-up in terms of the value of each pose, so you should use the version that you can perform most impressively. If you have excellent overall development, you can begin the pose in a vacuum position, then exhale and crunch down on your abdominals before moving on to the lat spread pose.

The degree of bend and hand supination that you use in your arms as you do a front double biceps shot depends largely on how well-developed your biceps and triceps have become

Tom Platz backstage with his Mr. Universe trophy in 1978. (*John Balik*)

and how evenly balanced your arm shape happens to be. Very few bodybuilders have the same shape to each arm, and you'll often see some of the better men holding each arm a little differently in order to make them both appear equal in shape and mass.

If you have a terrific biceps peak, you'll be better off bending your arms past a 90-degree angle and only half supinating your wrists. But if your biceps are not highly peaked, you may get a lot more out of holding them bent at right angles and completely supinating your wrists. Either way, I think it's more aesthetic to hold your elbows a bit upwards, so your upper arms are above a line parallel with the floor.

Leg position in all front poses depends on how well you have trained your thighs and calves. You'll get a better line to your body in a double biceps shot if you can point the toes of one foot slightly outward and bend that leg a few degrees, then extend the other leg a foot or so directly out to the side. However, you'll need highly developed thighs and calves in order to get away with this type of leg stance.

The best leg stance for the front double biceps and lat spread poses, should you not have highly developed legs, is to put one foot about four inches (10 cm) in front of the other, your toes on that foot pointed directly forward. And your back foot should be angled somewhat outward. Bend your legs slightly, or you won't be able to achieve maximum separation in your quads when you flex them.

Use the above leg position for your front lat spread pose. Place your hands on the sides of your waist in a position that will allow you to bend your arms at 90-degree angles as you perform the pose. With your palms towards the floor, hook your thumbs behind your waist and press your fists against the sides of your waist, no mean feat when your body is coated with a thin layer of oil, yet one that you can readily do with a bit of practice.

With your legs and arms correctly positioned, your next concern is holding your shoulders down. There's an inevitable tendency when first learning a front lat spread pose to allow the shoulders to ride upwards as you attempt to spread your lats. Unfortunately, it's very difficult to spread your lats in this position with your shoulders up. And raising your shoulders spoils the aesthetics of the pose.

Actually spreading your lats is partially a matter of controlling the muscle group so you can flare them outward and partially being able to spread your scapulae (shoulder blades) apart. This second ability can be fostered by working hard on shoulder flexibility exercises, particularly on towel dislocates (or a similar movement performed with a broomstick).

As you spread your lats and flex your legs, keep in mind that a front lat spread pose is also a chest shot, so you must additionally contract your pectorals and bring out every possible muscle striation. Finish off by tensing your arms, shoulders, and abdominals, and you'll soon have a first-class front lat spread pose.

Both side poses in Round One should be performed with your overall best side. Actually, doing each of these poses from a different side tips the judges off that you have balanced development on both sides of your body, but you'll see even the top Olympians performing both side shots from the same direction.

Almost universally, today's bodybuilders use a side leg stance in which they rest their bodyweight on a partially

bent back leg (the one away from the audience and judges), position their front foot slightly ahead of their back foot, bend the front leg and extend the foot, then flex all of the muscles on the outside of the leg towards the judging panel. This is a very effective way to display all of the cuts on the sides of your legs, particularly when you also pull the knee of your leg towards the audience across the midline of your body.

There are three other, albeit less popular, leg stances for side poses. In one, you bend both legs slightly and ex-

This unique shot was taken as Tom executed his famous back double-biceps pose at the 1980 Mr. Olympia in Sydney, Australia. (*Mike Neveux*)

tend the leg nearest the judges towards the rear, as though you had been caught halfway through a stride while walking down a beach. Second, you can place most of your weight on the slightly bent leg towards the judges, then extend your back leg to the rear and flex your calf and hamstring muscles on that leg. Finally, you can actually do a front leg stance with your upper body rotated to a side torso position. Let's say you're showing your left side in a chest pose. Your right foot will be somewhat ahead of your left, your toe pointed at a 90-degree angle with the front of the stage, and your left leg will be held straight and rotated so the front of it faces the judges and audience.

Regardless of which leg stance you choose, the manner in which you display your chest, shoulder, and arm development in a side chest pose is relatively standard from one bodybuilder to another. I'll describe it for a left-side

Tom Platz displays pleasing overall symmetry and incredible mass and muscularity in a double-biceps pose at the 1981 Mr. Olympia competition. (*John Balik*)

chest shot; if you happen to do the pose from the right side, simply reverse the instructions.

With your left palm held upwards, bend your left arm at approximately a 90-degree angle. Face your right palm downwards, either against your left hand or left wrist, and grasp hard enough with your right hand to keep your grip secure on your left hand or arm. Keeping your left forearm parallel to both the floor and the front of the stage, pull back with your left arm until your right forearm comes to rest firmly against your waist. Then with a moderate abdominal vacuum, hold your rib cage as high as you can without also elevating your shoulders, and flex all of the muscles on the left side of your arm and torso.

There are three tricks you can use in this pose. The first is to start with a vacuum shot and then crunch down into a contracted side chest pose, simultaneously lifting your left hip a couple of inches in order to help you get your intercostals to pop out in bold relief. The second trick—only to be used if you have weak forearm development—is to switch your left-hand position so your palm is downward as you do the pose. This de-emphasizes some of your biceps mass, but it definitely makes your forearms appear much more massive. And regardless of hand position, you should press your upper arm hard against the side of your torso in order to flatten it out and make it look bigger.

As you become more experienced as a poser, you can work on bringing out various striations in your pectorals and deltoids in both side poses. This is accomplished both by actually flexing the muscles to bring out a particular striation and by slightly altering your hand and arm positions.

Let's talk about foot and calf position in the two compulsory back poses. In the back double biceps shot, you must extend one foot or the other directly to the rear and flex the calf of that leg. Then during the back lat spread shot, most novice bodybuilders maintain this leg position. The better athletes tend to extend their other leg to the rear to show that they have equal calf development. I do my lat spread pose with my feet flat on the floor, a position in which I have found I can bring out some incredible calf striations.

To learn the flat-footed calf pose, start by rocking a bit forward so your weight is primarily on the balls of your feet. Then work on gripping the floor with your toes while attempting to flex your calves. At first, you probably won't be able to get any striations to show, but with some practice you'll begin to see an improvement. Eventually, you can put as many striations in your calves in this position as you can in your pectorals in many poses.

A back double biceps shot is very much like the front version of the pose, but with the addition of four little tricks. First, keep in mind that this pose displays your hamstrings, so you must keep your legs slightly bent and learn to fully tend your biceps femoris muscles. Failing to pose your leg biceps in *any* straight back shot reduces the effectiveness by at least 20 percent.

Three other tricks will help you to bring out more back details. First, be sure that you tense your abs as you do any back pose, because this helps to bring out the striations in the lumbar muscles of your lower back. Second, turn your head as far as you can to either side, which will add considerably to the details in your traps. And finally, attempt to rotate your upper-arm bones in their sockets by moving your wrists to the rear without also moving your elbows significantly past the midline of your

body. This last movement will greatly assist you in bringing out the muscular details of your middle back.

The back lat spread is very much like the front variation of the pose, except that you will round your torso forward and pull your elbows forward ahead of the midline of your torso. It's also very effective to start this pose by first pressing your shoulder blades together, then slowly spreading them as

Exceptional back development from head to toe. Have you ever seen a back as ripped up as Tom's? (*John Balik*)

An outstanding side triceps pose of Tom Platz. Note the excellence of his leg and arm development. (*John Balik*)

you spread your lats. This movement makes the width of your lat spread even more dramatic than it would be if you merely hit the shot with no introductory movement. And if your lower lats are well developed, you'll bring out some terrific striations in them when you press your shoulder blades together like this prior to hitting your full back lat spread pose.

To give right-handed bodybuilders a break, I'll tell you how to do the side triceps shot from the right side. And if you prefer to do the pose from the left side, simply reverse the directions.

First choose the type of leg stance you wish to use. If you used the stance with your audience-side foot ahead of your back foot, it would be ideal if you were to use the striding side leg stance for your triceps shot, since this leg position shows a greater overall degree of development. Indeed, in the women's compulsory poses, the IFBB and AFWB have decreed that exactly these differences in leg stance are required when doing the poses in Round One.

Your right arm will be held relatively straight and down at the side of your body, so reach across your back with your left hand and grasp your right wrist. In this position, your left forearm will rest across the small of your back, a secure position that allows you to push or pull as required with your right wrist against your braced left arm.

Some bodybuilders can bring out their triceps to a startling degree with their arms slightly bent, but most of you will find it easiest to fully tense your triceps with your right arm held straight. So press your right upper arm against the side of your torso to make it appear more thickly developed and tense your triceps for all you're worth. You'll probably find your triceps look best when your palms are towards your thighs, but try

Abdominal comparisons at the 1981 Mr. Olympia competition. (Front row, left to right) Dr. Franco Columbu (who won his second Mr. Olympia title in 1981), Tom Platz, and Chris Dickerson (who won the 1982 Mr. Olympia). (Back row) Ken Waller, Jusup Wilcosz, Roger Walker, Ed Corney, and Roy Callender. (*John Balik*)

also doing the pose with your palm either facing forward, towards the rear, or at some angle between these three major poles.

Keeping your right arm straight, push forward with your right wrist against your left hand to bring out your deltoid striations. Tense your pectorals and abdominals—particularly your obliques and intercostals—and you should have a very nice side triceps pose for the judges.

The final compulsory pose is the front abdominal and leg isolation shot. Start by setting your feet so one foot is about 12 inches (30 cm) in front of the other. Your back foot should be positioned with your toes angled outward, and the toes of your front foot should be pointed straight ahead. Bend your leg slightly and tense your quads to bring out thigh muscularity, simultaneously spreading and flexing your calves. Practice bending your leg to various angles as you flex your thigh muscles, because each new degree of bend produces a dif-

ferent look to your leg. One gives you plenty of sartorius and little frontal thigh muscle, while another gives you all frontal thigh and very little sartorius. Pick the one that looks best, or switch between the two leg stances in the midst of the pose.

Next place your hands behind your neck or head. Be certain to flex your biceps in this position, because failing to do so will detract considerably from how your upper body appears in this pose. Being sure to stand up as straight as possible, exhale and tense your abdominals. As long as you're concentrating on your rectus abdominis, intercostals and serratus muscles when you flex your abs, this will give you an excellent conclusion to your compulsory round of poses.

Round-Two Poses

In Round Two, you will stand semi-relaxed with your feet close together and your arms held at your sides facing the judges, with your left side towards the judging panel, facing away from the panel, and with your right side towards the judges. This round of posing reveals a great deal about your body symmetry and general muscle tone.

While you are supposed to stand "relaxed" in the poses from Round Two, everyone tends to keep at least their legs and abdominals fully flexed. You can also slightly flex every other muscle group in your body, the degree to which you flex depending on what the judges will allow at each individual competition. More and more frequently, however, all-out flexing is the name of the game in Round Two as well as in Round One.

Slight shifts of body position (legs, arms, torso, head, etc.) will make a big difference in how you look in each pose. It's impossible for me to tell you specifically what you need to work on, so you'll need to spend plenty of time in front of a mirror discovering for yourself what works best for your unique body.

Tom undergoes the scrutiny of the seven-member judging panel for the second round (semi-relaxed position) in recent competition. (*Mike Neveux*)

Round-Three Poses

In Round Three, unlike the first two compulsory rounds, you will present your own uniquely individual free-posing routine to your own choice of music. I pose to Christopher Cross's song, "Ride Like the Wind," and each of my own free poses is chosen to display my body at its best. In Round Three, you are at liberty—indeed, encouraged—to choose shots that highlight your strong points and camouflage the weak areas of your physique.

For some bodybuilders, the free-posing round becomes almost like a dance display, while for others, it is merely a chance to get out there and sock it to 'em with every supermuscular shot possible. The style of posing you choose will depend largely on your personality and on how completely you have developed your physique. My own style lies about halfway between dancer and boomer; I do all of the big poses, but I also make a conscious effort to assemble them with logical and aesthetic transitions between poses.

Before you begin working on your own free-posing routine, however, I strongly encourage you to attend as many competitions as possible, concentrating on how each competitor makes transitions between poses. And if you are unable for some reason to attend an actual high-level bodybuilding show, you can purchase films of most of the top bodybuilders going through their posing routines. These films are advertised in *Muscle & Fitness*, *MuscleMag International*, *Iron Man*, and most other bodybuilding journals.

The Posedown

If you are lucky enough to be in the top five after the first three rounds of posing, you will be included in the posedown at the end of the evening show. At the posedown, you can gain a final few precious points, so this part of the program becomes quite spirited and energetic. Often the competitors will change places in the lineup in order to compare themselves directly with their biggest competition.

There are two schools of thought regarding posedown conduct. In the first, you should feel complimented that a competitor singles you out as the one to beat, but you should remain aloof from it, merely going on with your planned program of your best poses. By moving next to you, he's admitted to himself (at least subconsciously) that you are in his league or better. And, you've already defeated him once he moves up to you.

In the second school of thought, you can go ahead and respond to your opponent. He hits you with a most muscular pose, and you shoot him right back with an even better version of the same stance. This attitude is highly applauded by the audience, who enjoy a spirited *mano-a-mano* duel between a pair of leading contenders.

Regardless of which path you do choose, however, be sure to have a short, 10- to 15-pose routine ready specifically for the posedown. Choose only those shots that show you at your absolute best, and hit them with a rapid cadence. Then if you want to jump into the fray against a specific competitor, go for it!

Posing Practice

It's not excessive to spend at least one hour per day practicing your posing, particularly not the last four to six weeks prior to a competition. About half of this time should be devoted to practicing Round One and Round Two poses, while the remainder of your practice time should be devoted to Round Three and the posedown.

Tom Platz and Ron Teufel engage in a spirited comparison of calf development at the 1978 Mr. America competition. (*Jimmy Caruso*)

One big mistake made by many novice bodybuilders is spending all of their time on perfecting a free-posing routine. As you will discover a bit later in this chapter, only one-third of your total score is awarded in Round Three. With the other two-thirds of your score coming in Round One and Round Two, it makes good sense to practice these rounds nearly as hard as the free-posing round.

I'd suggest that you establish a regular posing area in your home or apartment, one with relatively harsh lighting that reveals your physique's weak points in bold detail. Don't spend all of your time patting yourself on the back over your strong physical points, totally ignoring your weaknesses. It's a far better practice to take note of weak areas in your physique, then take action to improve them.

You'll need one main mirror, as well as a somewhat smaller mirror that can be set at an angle that reveals your back poses exactly as the judges will see them. There is absolutely no point in merely trying to feel out your back poses; you should be able to see them clearly enough to enable yourself to make improvements in body position.

Your first free-posing routines will probably be based heavily on the compulsory poses of Round One, although I feel that it's foolish for an experienced bodybuilder to repeat mandatory poses in his free-posing program. If you do the same poses, change them somehow. For example, I do a side triceps shot in my free-posing routine, but I do it in a kneeling position rather than standing.

Your first poses will come from imitating shots you have seen depicted in various muscle magazines, but you are strongly encouraged to develop your own unique "trademark" shots, those poses that you alone do best and which have become identified with your persona as a bodybuilder. For example, I've come to be known for my quadriceps isolation performed with my hands held behind my back. And the audience always loves to see me smooth my hair back with one hand as I transfer my hand to a position behind my head for a one-arm biceps shot. With time, dedication, and plenty of practice, you will develop your own trademark shots.

After careful observation, I've concluded that a good novice-level posing routine will consist of 10–12 shots. Still, you'll see plenty of young guys trying to pull off the 30-pose routine of a seasoned Olympian, striking only 10 great shots

and letting 20 bad poses overwhelm the good poses. It's far better to do a small number of great poses than many mediocre shots, then gradually increase the number of poses in your routine as your body becomes more mature.

It's not excessive to begin developing your free-posing program—as well

Tom performs the first pose of his famous "hair" one-arm biceps shot. . . .

. . . the second sequence . . .

If you're having trouble coming up with good transitions between poses, I strongly suggest that you hire the services of a dance instructor or choreographer for a few hours. Such a man or woman can do wonders for your posing ability, and they can be located by calling local dance studios, listed in the yellow pages of your telephone directory.

. . . and the final pose. (*Mike Neveux*)

as to begin practicing stances for the first two rounds—at least three months ahead of a competition. This will give you plenty of time in which to develop masterful individual poses, choose music, and choreograph a routine with artistic transitions between poses (again, these transitions can be learned from watching the posing routines of many other bodybuilders).

Platz has gradually improved his upper-body development to equal or better any bodybuilder competing today. (*Mike Neveux*)

Over months and years of posing practice, observing others onstage, and actually being onstage yourself, you will learn little tricks of the trade that will endear you to both the audience and judges. And these tricks will give you an indispensable quality—*charisma*. Very little can defeat a bodybuilder in top shape who also has an effective posing skill and a high degree of charisma.

Personal Appearance

While the quality is not directly scored in a bodybuilding competition, your personal appearance (tan, skin tone, posing suit, grooming, etc.) can have a bearing on the final outcome of your competition. As a result, I strongly suggest that you take steps to optimize your personal appearance.

Tanning

I've always been noted for my dark tan onstage at competitions, a tan which makes my physique appear both harder and healthier. I have always relied solely on a natural tanning process, being out in the sun at least three or four months prior to a Mr. Olympia competition.

You should allow at least six weeks in order to attain a deep, natural tan. Blitzing a tan, and burning your skin in the process, is counterproductive because a sunburn will draw water into your skin, making you appear much smoother than you actually are. It's much better to begin tanning early with short periods of exposure to the sun, then gradually work up exposure time as your skin darkens.

I'd suggest starting with 10–15 minutes of sun exposure on both the front and back of your body. I prefer to lie out between the hours of 10:30 A.M. and 2:00 P.M., the hours of most direct sun exposure in Los Angeles. However, if your skin is rather fair, you should begin sun exposure before or after this peak intensity time.

Fair-skinned individuals (if your skin is dark, you may not even need to worry about a tan) should also consider using a sunscreen on their skin as they build up exposure time. Frequently reapplied, a sunscreen filters out harmful, burning rays and permits the tanning rays to reach your skin. Sunscreens of varying strengths can be purchased at any pharmacy.

I use a vegetable-oil coating on my skin when exposing myself to the sun. Commonly used oils—all available in bulk at health-food stores—are almond, avocado, olive, and safflower. The oil keeps my skin soft and supple, as well as completely moisturized. And to further moisturize my skin when heavily into sunbathing, I rub in Nivea cream both in the morning after my shower and at night before retiring.

In addition to lying on your back and stomach, you should ultimately lie at various other angles in order to ensure an even tan over your entire body. And, you'll need to hold your hands above your head while lying on your back in order to tan your skin under your arms and along the sides of your torso.

I prefer lying in the sun both for the depth of tan that results from sun exposure, and also because regular sunbathing tends to dehydrate my skin, making it appear as though it's painted on my body over my muscles. And the hotter the sun the last few days before a show, the better I like it for its skin-dehydrating characteristics. Therefore, it's not uncommon for me to pack my bags and jet off to Acapulco, Mexico, for a few days just prior to competing in a Mr. Olympia show!

If you are unable to achieve a deep, natural tan, you can still safely get a good tan by lying in sun beds. Some authorities argue that such a salon tan is actually safer because the lights in a sun bed don't have the harmful, burning rays of natural sun, only the tanning ultraviolet rays. Additionally, a sun-bed tan is almost invariably quite even. Still, I prefer and recommend attaining a natural tan through sunbathing.

The worst type of tan is one achieved through chemical means, either in the form of makeup or from one of the formerly popular bronzing creams that briefly turn your skin a sort of sickly yellow or orange. If you must resort to a chemical tan, I suggest using one of the tan-colored makeups available at women's cosmetic counters at large department stores. These makeup preparations come in the form of a fine powder which you can rub into your skin and over which you can apply any vegetable-based oil with minimum streaking. Two popular trade names for this type of makeup are Indian Earth and Beverly Hills Dirt.

Grooming

You simply *must* have a fresh haircut and shave prior to any competition, so you appear as wholesome and clean-cut as

At the 1978 Mr. America competition, Tom Platz compares back development with Mr. USA Ron Teufel (left). (*Jimmy Caruso*)

possible onstage. There's nothing wrong with wearing your hair a bit long, unless it is so long that it obscures the muscularity of your upper back or shoulders. Just make sure that your hair—as well as a beard or moustache—is well groomed and neat.

I strongly suggest that you have your hair professionally cut and styled, because a professional stylist can create the most flattering hairstyle possible for your general features. It's okay in many respects to go to the corner barber shop, but close to a contest I'd rather spend a few extra dollars to have my hair professionally styled.

You will also need to shave off all body hair to keep it from obscuring any of your hard-earned muscular development. This should be done the first time with a safety razor while in a hot bath, then touched up each three or four days with an electric razor. This procedure will allow plenty of time for inadvertent nicks and cuts to heal up before you step onstage for your competition.

Posing Suit

Choose a solid-color suit that complements your own general coloring and is cut to display maximum muscularity. You can find many advertisements for posing suits on the pages of *Muscle & Fitness* and other bodybuilding magazines, or you can have one custommade. Never wear one with a pattern or more than one color; they're too distracting. You want your muscles, not your suit, to be what the audience and judges most remember about you the day after a bodybuilding show.

Similarly, you should avoid wearing jewelry, except a wedding ring, onstage. Any large or garish display of personal jewelry would also distract from your overall appearance.

Oiling

In order to create the three-dimension effect resulting from a posing light shining on your body, you must use a light coating of oil on your skin. And it's best to use a vegetable oil (the same one as you use for tanning would be just fine), since the vegetable oil sinks into your pores and later slowly emerges as you perspire onstage posing. Petroleum-based oils simply lie on your skin and soak up much more light than they reflect.

It's a bit difficult to get your oil right the first time out of the chute, so I'd suggest that you use an "oiler" who can help you oil up and then stand in the audience and make corrections in the amount of oil you are using each time you come off the stage. You'll need to replenish your oil job every time offstage anyway, so get used to the idea.

If anything, it's best to keep your oil job on the light side at first, being sure to rub the oil deeply into your skin. Oil lying on your skin will drip and run, which can be unsightly onstage. And oil drips can ruin the posing suit, the stage floor, and the floor of the dressing rooms backstage.

Pumping Up

You've no doubt noticed that your muscles "pump up"—become larger as a result of blood rushing into them during exercise—after you've done a few sets of an exercise. Bodybuilders use this phenomenon to advantage onstage by pumping up backstage prior to being judged. By judiciously pumping up, you can make a weak muscle group appear somewhat stronger than it actually is.

There will usually be weights backstage that can be used when pumping up, but you should always have a program of calisthenics to do if weights aren't available. Start your pumping session with a general, full-body warm-up consisting of one or two sets for each muscle group, and keep your reps in the range of 15–20 on all sets. Finish your pumping session with two or three sets each for one or two weak body parts prior to going onstage. You might also profit from one more set for each of these muscle groups each time you go backstage, just as long as you don't totally spoil your oil job by lying down on a bench to pump up again.

Be wary of overpumping, which can make a muscle appear smooth and bloated. And if you find after a period of time that going through your posing routine a couple of times is a sufficient warm-up, then you should avoid any direct pumping up.

Tom performs chins behind neck a few days prior to the Mr. Olympia contest. Look at the amazing details of muscular definition. (*John Balik*)

Tom Platz (left) poses for second place in the short class at the 1977 Mr. America competition. Ron Teufel (center) won the class. Andreas Cahling is at right. (*Bill Reynolds*)

The Competition

There's quite a bit that goes on at a competition that you should pay attention to. And it would be best if you could observe several competitions—both in front of the stage and backstage—prior to actually jumping into your own first competition.

First make sure that you're ready for a particular level of competition by observing the contestants in similar-level shows. *Be objective!* You've never seen anything as embarrassing as someone entered in a show for which he or she is simply not ready.

You should also check the entry blank for an upcoming show to be sure that you meet all of the eligibility requirements (age, competitive experience, area of residence, and so forth). You can obtain entry blanks by writing or phon-

Tom winning the 1978 IFBB Mr. Universe title at Acapulco, Mexico. He weighed a solid 198 pounds and out-muscled 30 international contestants. (*Jimmy Caruso*)

ing promoters of shows listed in the "Coming Events" columns of various bodybuilding magazines.

How You Are Judged

There will be seven judges at each competition you enter, and each of them will give you a placing rank in each of the three posing/judging rounds. You will be ranked according to how good you are in each of these three rounds, and your placing is your score for that round. Placings in all three rounds are later totalled, with the athlete recording the lowest score declared champion.

While you will be given seven placing scores in each round, only five of them will be totalled up to result in your round score. To prevent favoritism of any sort, both the high and low scores given to you in a round are dropped before the remaining five scores are totalled.

In Round Three, you will pose individually; but in the first two rounds, you will be compared directly with other bodybuilders. In the initial two rounds, you will first come out by yourself, then later will be called out of a line-up for comparisons in groups of two to five bodybuilders. This gives the judges a chance to see how you stack up with other athletes near your own level of excellence before they are required to score each competitor.

In Round One and Round Two, you must be very alert to the judges' commands. You'll look like a complete fool if you happen to turn to the right when everyone else in your group has correctly turned to the left, yet you'll see this happen frequently at a competition prejudging.

About 98 percent of your score will be awarded in the first three rounds of posing/judging, but I've seen close competitions decided in the posedown. The posedown is only worth a small part of your total score, but it *can* vault you past a close competitor and into a higher placing. So give it all you have.

You'll be able to easily observe how a competition is judged by merely attending several of them prior to entering your first show. However, it's much more difficult to get backstage and see some of the petty "psyching" that goes on between the various competitors. That's something you usually have to experience for yourself. Just don't get carried away by what someone says to you backstage. He'll just be saying it to undermine your confidence, so don't get shaken by this silly psyching game.

Defining a Winner

No doubt you have wondered what it actually takes to win a high-level bodybuilding championship. A winning bodybuilder will have each of the following seven qualities in abundance:

1. Quality muscle mass, free of both intramuscular and surface body fat.
2. Well-balanced physical proportions, with no outstanding strong or weak muscle groups.
3. Maximum possible muscle mass, given the previous two provisos.
4. Effective posing ability, including obvious personal charisma.
5. Perfect grooming, including good skin tone and the correct choice of posing suit.
6. The intelligence, initiative, and willingness to learn everything possible about all aspects of the sport of bodybuilding, and particularly an ability to learn from past mistakes.
7. A winning mental attitude.

10 The Learning Process

This is our last chapter together, so it's time that I give you a brief lecture on bodybuilding public relations. There's nothing wrong with having a great physique. Indeed, much of the public these days will praise you for looking and being physically strong. However, it's a real mistake to attempt to force yourself—mentally and/or physically—down anyone's throat.

Have you ever seen a young guy who's developed a little bit of muscle and struts around in public with a skintight T-shirt (even in subfreezing temperatures), every muscle in his body tensed to the limit? It's a ridiculous sight, isn't it? This behavior reflects badly on the character of the man who makes such a mistake, and it reflects badly on the sport of bodybuilding.

It's far better to dress conservatively. Believe me, your muscles will show through clothing two inches thick. And everyone has respect for men who show their character through positive action rather than loud-mouthed bragging. Make a good choice for yourself and your sport.

This chapter discusses the learning process in bodybuilding, a process that I consider to be quite important to your development. If you are unable to learn everything possible about your sport—and particularly if you can't learn from your mistakes—you won't have much of a chance at succeeding competitively. The best bodybuilders are open to new knowledge and particularly sensitive to biofeedback signals transmitted by their bodies.

Instinctive Training

One of the most crucial factors in bodybuilding is the development of an instinctive sense of what works for your body. It will be difficult for you to believe this if you're still new to bodybuilding, but all of the champion bodybuilders can instinctively sense which dietary and training stimuli are working well or poorly for them. In turn, this instinctive training ability allows the champs to immediately abandon faulty techniques in favor of those that bring more immediate results, saving years of false experimentation in the process.

Bodybuilding really *is* a grand experiment in which you test a huge variety of stimuli in your body lab, read the results of each experiment (through training instinct), and apply what you learn to build your body more quickly. For example, you can learn which rep range is best for training your deltoids in the off-season merely by spending a couple of weeks experimenting with sets of varying reps. At least, you can quickly learn which rep range works best if you've correctly developed your instinctive ability.

How is training instinct developed? It takes several months of monitoring various biofeedback data and relating it to the training variables.

Muscle pump—the tight, blood-congested feeling in a muscle following a good workout—is the one piece of biofeedback datum used by all bodybuilders to determine if a particular exercise, set-rep scheme, training program, or full workout is of value. If a routine of five sets of ten reps each for bench presses, inclines, and parallel bar dips blows your pecs up like balloons, you know that you've discovered a routine that works well for your chest. It's that simple.

The following are other common pieces of bodybuilding biofeedback that you can relate to your workouts and diet as you develop instinctive training ability: muscle soreness, obvious changes in muscle mass and density, changes in anthropometric measurements, increases or decreases in workout poundages, presence or absence of body fatigue, changes in body fat percentage, relative ability to concentrate on a muscle being trained, speed of recovery between sets (as well as between workouts), relative energy levels, and relative levels of training enthusiasm. With a little thought, I'm sure that you can come up with many more bodybuilding biofeedback data.

One of the best ways to achieve instinctive training ability is to maintain a detailed training and nutrition log. Simply use a notebook or bound diary to record every exercise, the sets and reps you perform in your workouts, what you eat and when, and any other observations of mental approach and mood that could possibly have a bearing on the speed at which you improve as a bodybuilder.

In the early stages of your development, I'd suggest that you include body measurements (upper arms, forearms, chest expanded, waist, thighs, and calves) at monthly intervals. After six months to a year, however, you won't notice quick changes in these measurements unless you are actually gaining weight. Past that point, I think it's much better to include monthly or bimonthly photos of yourself in a variety of poses. Simply glue or tape them into your diary for a visual record of your progress.

Co-author Bill Reynolds (left) interviews Tom Platz backstage prior to the 1980 Mr. Olympia in Sydney, Australia. (*John Balik*)

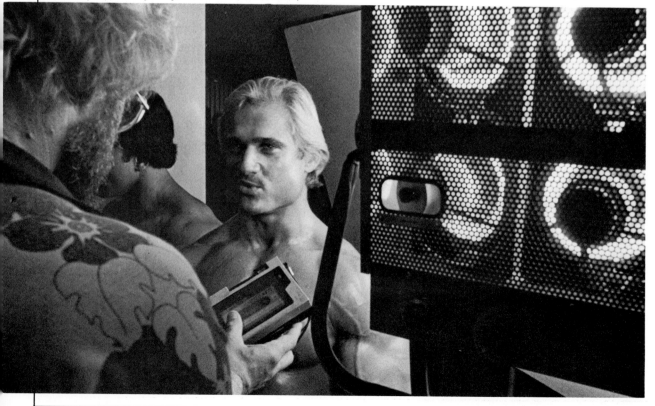

My workouts are both different from and similar to those of Arnold Schwarzenegger and Mike Mentzer. Arnold won't make gains on Mike's routines, and Mike won't make gains on Arnold's. I won't make good gains on either man's programs, but through experimentation and use of training instinct, I've determined that certain facets of each man's routines work well for me. And in the end, I've come up with a training philosophy that incorporates the best of each type of program.

I've often said in this book that there are no definites or absolutes in bodybuilding, that I can only tell you what *should* work for you, and that you can only know what works through your own experiments. Without instinctive training ability, you won't be able to learn from your experiments. Therefore, training instinct becomes one of the most crucial factors in your formula for bodybuilding success.

Learning from Mistakes

One characteristic of successful bodybuilders is that they are always eager to learn from their own mistakes. Knowledge is power, and they seek knowledge at every turn. They thrive and grow on what they can learn, both as human beings and as bodybuilders.

Many unsuccessful bodybuilders whom I've observed training at literally hundreds of gyms worldwide are what I call *closed-system people.* I'm sure that you know a few of them yourself, the type of person who feels that he or she knows absolutely everything about his or her sport. In contrast, I firmly believe that I can learn something valuable from every individual I encounter in my travels and everyday life. Closed-system people are really experts at nothing, but they convince themselves that they are.

And that's a sure road to failure in competitive bodybuilding.

I strongly urge you to become an *open-system bodybuilder,* because that is one of the best routes to success. Be open to criticism and suggestions from everyone. If you are, you'll find that some of the most profound things are said by the most unlikely people. Closed-system bodybuilders lose out on this type of invaluable learning experience.

You'd be surprised at how few competitive bodybuilders are able to learn from their past mistakes. They lose show after show by making the same fundamental mistakes over and over. You *must* learn from your mistakes as well as from your successes if you intend to become a champion. And don't get down on yourself for making mistakes. Everyone makes mistakes, and you wouldn't be able to appreciate your successes if you didn't fail now and then.

Sources of Knowledge

Without a doubt, personal contact with the champions of the sport—the type that you only get by training at a place like Gold's Gym or the World Gym—is the best way to learn the fine points about bodybuilding. You can ask the champs to help solve your training problems. However, many bodybuilding enthusiasts live in smaller towns, away from the big cities that attract top bodybuilders. And even if you live in a big city, there may be no champions in the area.

If you don't have frequent, direct contact with champion bodybuilders, the best way to increase your knowledge of the bodybuilding process is to read. I have well over 100 bodybuilding and weight-training books in my personal library, and just in English I'm sure there are nearly 200 books in print that have a direct bearing on increased knowledge of bodybuilding. Check your local book-store or library for titles.

There are also many scientific books that yield valuable information about areas such as anatomy, kinesiology, physiology, psychology, biochemistry, and biomechanics that are related to the bodybuilding process. It takes intelligence and a willingness to learn in order to read and profit from scientific texts, but I feel it's essential to understand all the complexities of the sport of bodybuilding.

In your readings, you will receive much conflicting data. The same will hold true in conversations with top bodybuilders and other athletes. Again, this is mostly a matter of bodybuilding not being an exact science; every bodybuilder learns things a bit differently, and he or she explains them differently as well. But if you come across some piece of information that is explained one way in one text and a different way in ten others, I think you can feel free to pick the majority view.

Magazines are a valuable source of information, particularly of current knowledge that won't be published yet in books for a year or more. I'm partial to *Muscle & Fitness* and *Flex* magazines, which exclusively publish articles that I write. However, I read *MuscleMag International*, *Iron Man*, *Muscle Training Illustrated*, *Muscular Development*, and many other bodybuilding magazines in a constant effort to improve and update my knowledge of training, diet, and mental approach.

A last source of printed information is the large number of training courses that various champion bodybuilders have published. In many cases, these courses contain information that has already appeared in the various bodybuilding magazines, but some champs—myself included—have taken care to re-serve some of the secrets just for our courses. For the names of some on the market, you need simply consult the many advertisements carried in *Muscle & Fitness* magazine.

You may have the opportunity to talk with a champion at a bodybuilding competition at which he or she is guest-posing. You'll find us easy to approach, so don't be afraid to ask a question or two. However, you'll often be forced to contend with the masses of other fans who demand equal time.

If you're lucky, the competition promoter or a gym owner in your area will also have engaged the guest poser to present a training seminar before or after the day of a show. Seminars offer an excellent way to meet and talk with champion bodybuilders, and you should take advantage of every seminar presented near you. You will be charged a modest fee to attend a seminar, but what you can learn at one of these sessions is invaluable.

Finally, some bodybuilders offer personal coaching, either in person at the gym where they train, or via cassette tapes through the mail. Simply ask your favorite bodybuilder in person if he does personal coaching, then determine his fees. Or look in the mail-order ads of various champions to see if they do personal coaching through the mail.

I'm also a big believer in learning from athletes in other sports and physical disciplines (i.e., dance, martial arts, etc.). Each of these athletic individuals has an approach to his or her sport or activity that has made him or her successful. You can determine which factors will benefit you by either talking with such an individual or reading his or her books. An open-system bodybuilder always takes advantage of these opportunities to increase his knowledge of the sport.

Drugs and the Competitive Edge

All bodybuilders are constantly trying to gain an edge on their competition. This is one reason why drug usage is so rampant in the sport. It's unfortunate that many individuals try to take the easy way out with drugs rather than becoming bodybuilders who prize knowledge and hard work in their routes to success.

Here is one last Tom Platz maxim for bodybuilding success: An intelligent and knowledgeable bodybuilder always has the edge over others who fail to develop an intellect and seek knowledge.

You already know that I believe drugs are overemphasized and overused in bodybuilding, that you can actually make progress more quickly when you don't resort to anabolic steroids. I firmly believe that learning everything you possibly can about bodybuilding will give you an edge even over those athletes who rely heavily on steroids and other bodybuilding drugs.

Our Last Set Together

We have come to the end of our discussion of competitive bodybuilding. One thing I would like to leave you with is an appreciation of being a *feeler* rather than a *lifter* in your workouts. Everyone is so concerned with numbers—how many, how much, how fast. I seldom even pay attention to the actual poundage I am using in each exercise. You should be more concerned with feelings, with the sheer joy of movement, with the way your muscles feel as you train them.

You should control your training; your training should never control you. Bodybuilding should add to the enjoyment of your life. It shouldn't be your complete life. Training should be fun. Make sure you keep it that way!

Tom guest-posing at the 1982 Russ Warner Classic in San Jose, California. (*Terry*)

Index

abdomen
   basic and isolation exercises, 16*illus*
   level-one off-season workout, 84
   level-two off-season workout, 85
abdominal shot, front, 171
aerobics, 96-97
amino acids, 29
anabolic steroids, 93, 189
appearance, personal, 176-180
arm(s)
   level-one off-season workout, 84
   level-two off-season workout, 85

back
   double biceps shot, 168-169
   lat spread, 169-170
   level-one off-season workout, 84
   level-two off-season workout, 85
   poses, 168-169
   trisets, 97
barbell
   bent rows, 56-57
   curls, 70-71
   preacher curls, 140-141
   triceps extension, 74
   wrist curls, 78-79, 89
Basal Metabolic Rate (BMR), 154
basic exercises, vs. isolation, 15-16*illus*
belts, weightlifting, 37, 57
bench presses, 58-59
   close-grip, 142-143
bent laterals, 138-139
bent rows, barbell, 56-57
biceps femoris, 48
BMR (Basal Metabolic Rate), 154
bodybuilding books, 187-188
boredom, mental, 35
burnout series, 17
burns, 26, 77, 99

cable crossovers, 132-133
calf (calves)
   basic and isolation exercises, 16*illus*
   flat-footed pose, 169
   machine toe raises, 88, 91
   seated machine toe raises, 91
   seated raises, 116-117
   standing machine toe raises, 91
   standing raises, 50-51
Callard, Roger, 21*illus*
cheating reps, 15, 23, 25
chest
   level-one off-season workout, 84
   level-two off-season workout, 85
   trisets, 97
chins
   close-grip, 126-127
   front, 54
   narrow-grip, 87
circuit training, 95*illus*
closed-system people, 187
close-grip bench press, 142-143
close-grip chins, 126-127
Columbu, Franco, 13
competition, 165-183, 181-183
competitive edge, and drugs, 189
concentration, 161-162
continuous tension, 98-99
cross-bench pullovers, 22*illus*, 64-65, 87
crossovers, cable, 132-133
crunches, 150-151
curls
   barbell, 70-71
   barbell preacher, 140-141
   dumbbell, 72
   leg, 91, 114-115
   seated dumbbell, 88-89
cytotoxic diet, 108-109

deadlifts, 14*illus*, 52-53, 87-88
   stiff-legged, 53
deltoids
   basic and isolation exercises, 16*illus*
   trisets, 97-98
descending sets, 99-100
diet
   cytotoxic, 108-109
   importance of, 22
   low-carbohydrate, 107-108
   low-fat, 105-107
   Tom Platz's off-season, 32-33
digestive supports, 30-31
dips
   parallel bar, 60-61, 88, 102*illus*, 144-145
   reverse-grip, 89
distress, 38-39
diversity of interests, 163
double-split routines, 102-103
drugs, and the competitive edge, 189
dumbbells
   bent laterals, 87
   cross-bench pullovers, 87
   curls, 72

incline curls, 40*illus*
incline flyes, 88, 99*illus*
incline presses, 88, 128-129
one-arm wrist curls, 146-147
seated curls, 88-89
seated presses, 134-135
side laterals, 68-69
standard side laterals, 88

erector spinae, exercises, 16*illus*
eustress, 38-39
extended-sets training system, 27
extensions, leg, 46-47, 91, 100*illus*

failure, training to, 22-23
fatigue, and sticking points, 35
fats, 105
Ferrigno, Lou, 12, 13, 20
five-day workout, 12-13
flat-bench flyes, 62-63
flat-footed calf pose, 169
flexibility training, 39-40
flyes
   dumbbell incline, 88, 99*illus*
   flat-bench, 62-63
   pec-deck, 130-131
forced reps, 25
   negative reps, 101
forearm exercises, 16*illus*
four-day workout cycle, 19, 154, 155
Fox, Bertil, 13
free weights, vs. machines, 19-20
front
   abdominal and leg isolation shot, 171
   chins, 54
   double biceps pose, 165-166
   lat pulldown, 54
   lat spread pose, 165, 166-167
   leg stance, 167-168

Gajda, Bob, 95
galactose intolerance, 31
gastrocnemius, 50
giant sets, 97-98
goal setting, 162
grooming, 178-179

hack squats, 91, 112-113
hamstrings, 48
hand supination, 41, 72
Haney, Lee, 13
hard gainers, 20-22
heavy vs. light training, 17
hyperextensions, 124-125

IFBB
   doping controls, 93
   posing system, 165-173
incline exercises
   dumbbell presses, 88, 128-129
   flyes, 88
   sit-ups, 24*illus*, 88
individualized routines, 37-38
injuries, 15, 41
instinctive training, 87, 185-187
intensity, 86

increasing, 94
maximum training, 102
training, 86
isolation exercises, 15-16*illus*

joint wraps, 37
judging, 183

knees, and squatting, 45

laterals
bent, 138-139
dumbbell bent, 87
side dumbbell, 68-69
standing side, dumbbell, 88
latissimus dorsi, exercises, 16*illus*
lat-machine pulldowns, 122-123
lat spread
back, 169-170
front, 165, 166-167
layoffs, 38
learning process, 185-189
left-side chest shot, 168
leg(s)
bench raises, 82
curls, 48-49, 91
extension, 46-47, 91, 100*illus*
isolation shot, 171
level-one off-season workout, 84
level-two off-season workout, 85
standing curls, 114-115
level-four workout, 154-155
level-one off-season workout, 84
level-three workout, 154
level-two off-season workout, 84-85
light vs. heavy training, 17
low-carbohydrate diet, 107-108
low-fat diet, 105-107

machine(s)
leg-curl, 48-49
leg-extension, 46
standing presses, 87
vs. free weights, 19-20
magazines, bodybuilding, 188
maximum training, 102
mental approach, 157-163
mental boredom, 35
mental intensity, 13
Mentzer, Mike, 27
military presses, 66-67
milk, and weight gain, 31
mind, 94, 157-163
mistakes, learning from, 187
moisturization, skin, 41
muscle-priority training, 11-13
muscle pump, 185

narrow-grip chins, 87
negative reps, 100-101

off-season
diet, 29-33
goals, 43
level-one workout, 84
level-two workout, 84-85
objectives, 11

power training, 13-15
Tom Platz's routine, 85-91
training factors, 35-41
oiling, 179
open-system people, 187
optimum physical condition, 103
overtraining, 26-27

parallel bar dips, 60-61, 88, 102*illus*, 144-145
partial reps, 86
partners, training, 36-37
peak contraction, 98
pec-deck flyes, 130-131
pectoral exercises, 16*illus*
Peripheral Heart Action (PHA), 95-96*illus*
PER (protein efficiency ratio), 29
personal appearance, 176-180
PHA training, 95-96*illus*
physical condition, optimum, 103
Platz, Tom, 8*illus*, 10*illus*, 12*illus*, 17*illus*, 28*illus*, 34*illus*, 36*illus*, 42*illus*, 43*illus*, 90*illus*, 92*illus*, 104*illus*, 110*illus*, 156*illus*, 159*illus*, 164*illus*, 169*illus*
at Mr. Olympia contest (1981), 168*illus*
at Mr. Universe contest (1980), 167*illus*
doing cross-bench pullovers, 22*illus*
doing deadlifts, 14*illus*
doing incline dumbbell curls, 40*illus*
doing incline flyes, 99*illus*
doing incline sit-ups, 24*illus*
doing leg extensions, 100*illus*
doing parallel bar dips, 102*illus*
doing presses behind neck, 23*illus*
doing seated pulley rows, 27*illus*
doing wrist curls, 89*illus*
extended-sets training system, 27
off-season diet, 32-33
off-season routine, 85-91
on leg-extension machine, 19*illus*
precontest program, 155
prior to 1980 Mr. Olympia show, 32*illus*
riding a bike, 39*illus*
with Mr. Universe trophy (1978), 166*illus*
with Roger Callard, 21*illus*
posedown, 172-173
posing
practice, 173-176
round-one, 165-171
round-three, 172
round-two, 171-172
posing suit, 179
positive thinking, 157-158
power-rack training, 26
preacher curls, 140-141
precontest
diet, 105-109
exercises and routines, 111-155

supplementation, 108
training tips, 93-103
presses
bench, 58-59
close-grip bench, 142-143
dumbbell seated, 134-135
incline dumbbell, 128-129
machine standing, 87
protein
complete, 29
for weight-gain diet, 29-30
incomplete, 29
protein efficiency ratio (PER), 29
supplements, 31
psychological edge, 162
pulldowns
front lat, 54
lat-machine, 122-123
pulley
pushdowns, 76-77, 89
rows, seated, 27*illus*, 118-119
pullovers, cross-bench, 22*illus*, 64-65, 87
pumping up, 17, 179-180
pump, muscle, 185
pushdowns, pulley, 76-77, 89
Pyramid system, 13-15

quadriceps, 46-47
quality training, 94-96

reps
partial, 86
single, 15
rest-pause training, 101
reverse-grip dips, 89
Roman chair sit-ups, 80-81
Round-one
judging, 183
posing, 165-171
Round-three
judging, 183
posing, 172
Round-two
judging, 183
posing, 171-172
routines
double-split, 102-103
five-day split, 18
four-day cycle, 19
four-day split, 18
individualized, 37-38
six-day off-season split, 19
split, 17-19
rows
barbell bent, 56-57
pulley, 27*illus*, 118-119
T-bar, 120-121
upright, 136-137

Schwarzenegger, Arnold, 13, 20, 27, 99, 158, 162
self-actualization, 159-161
self-confidence, 162-163
set(s), descending, 99-100
shoulder(s)
level-one off-season workout, 84
level-two off-season workout, 85

side
bends, 88
bends with seated twists, 152-153
dumbbell laterals, 68-69
poses, 167
triceps shot, 170-171
sit-ups, 148-149
incline, 88
Roman chair, 80-81, 88
six-day-per-week training, 155
skin
moisturization, 41
oiling, 179
tanning, 177-178
social life, 163
split routines, 17-19
squats, 44-45
full, 90
hack, 91, 112-113
steroids, 93, 189
sticking points, 35-36
stiff-legged deadlifts, 53
stress management, 38-39
stretching, 39-40, 88
stretch marks, 40-41

stripping method, 99-100
supersets, 25-26
supination, 41, 72
supplementation, precontest, 108

tanning, 177-178
T-bar rows, 120-121
tension, continuous, 98-99
thigh biceps, 48
thighs
basic and isolation exercises,
16illus
trisets, 97
thinking, positive, 157-158
toe raises
calf machine, 88
seated calf machine, 91
standing calf machine, 91
training intensity, 86
maximum, 102
training partners, 36-37
training programs, 20
training to failure, 22-23
trapezius exercises, 16illus

triceps
barbell extensions, 74
shot, 170-171
trisets, 97-98
twists, 88
seated side bends, 152-153

upright rows, 136-137

variable routines, 38
Viator, Casey, 13
visualization, 159-161
vitamins, 31-32
B complex, 32
E, 41
precontest supplementation, 108

weak points, identification of, 11
weight-gain diet, 29-32
Wilson, Scott, 13
winners, defining, 183
wraps, joint, 37
wrist curls, 89illus
barbell, 78-79, 89
one-arm dumbbell, 146-147